M000074731

Power and Possibility

Elizabeth Alexander

Power and Possibility

ESSAYS, REVIEWS, AND INTERVIEWS

THE UNIVERSITY OF MICHIGAN PRESS

Ann Arbor

Copyright © by Elizabeth Alexander 2007
All rights reserved
Published in the United States of America by
The University of Michigan Press
Manufactured in the United States of America
∞ Printed on acid-free paper

2010   2009   2008   2007   4   3   2   1

No part of this publication may be reproduced,
stored in a retrieval system, or transmitted in any form
or by any means, electronic, mechanical, or otherwise,
without the written permission of the publisher.

A CIP catalog record for this book is available from the British Library.

Library of Congress Cataloging-in-Publication Data

Alexander, Elizabeth, 1962–
    Power and possibility : essays, reviews, and interviews /
Elizabeth Alexander.
        p. cm. — (Poets on poetry)
    Includes bibliographical references.
    ISBN-13: 978-0-472-09937-5 (cloth : alk. paper)
    ISBN-10: 0-472-09937-X (cloth : alk. paper)
    ISBN-13: 978-0-472-06937-8 (pbk. : alk. paper)
    ISBN-10: 0-472-06937-3 (pbk. : alk. paper)
    1. American poetry—African American authors—History and
criticism.   2. American poetry—20th century—History and
criticism.   3. African Americans—Intellectual life—20th century.
4. African American poets—Interviews.   I. Title.

PS310.N4A43   2007
811'.509896073—dc22   2007008824

Contents

III. Talking

Introduction

In a recent discussion I heard myself saying, "Reading is experience, as digging a ditch or having a baby or going to Paris is experience." I was speaking of my own journey in particularly interesting communities of letters. This is not to say that I have spent the last twenty-five years curled up in an overstuffed chair; rather, I have been studying, writing, reading, teaching, puzzling over, and attempting to illuminate words that have in some way happened to me.

It has long been my way to be the young person listening at the feet of elders. I have learned much in that manner, and in large part my writing has been an attempt to make solid something from that rich and gorgeous evanescence. I have seen, also, much that is not recorded and can be easily lost. No longer the ingenue, I see how this listening led me to work that is in keeping with the historical recovery that has been such an important part of African-American and women's history over the last several generations. I have thought about why I move toward culture and its offerings as well as what I have struggled against. The mysteries of art and the bounty of black creative expression have changed its receivers and changed me.

These essays together argue for the power and possibility that are the legacies of twentieth-century culture. The past century of world wars, class stratification and upheaval, gender revolution, and "the color line" was also marked by cultural movements of tremendous significance. With each movement comes its artifacts: its poems, paintings, dances, and other creative expressions of the times. In the latter part of the twentieth century I wrote looking back and forward concurrently to the possibilities that culture can envision. "Where there is no vision, the people perish" comes first from the Bible, but the saying became a talisman for me when I saw it inscribed on James Hampton's remarkable "vernacular" sculpture *Throne Of The Third Heaven Of The Nations Millenium General Assembly* in Washington, D.C. The work collected here ranges from 1990 to 2006 and mostly looks at African-American culture, much of it created by women, through a critical lens with poetic sensibility.

I have always been fascinated by writers who work in more than one genre. I first wrote fiction and then worked at the *Washington Post*—my hometown paper—in 1984 just after college. There soon came a clear moment when I could feel myself bumping up against the limits of daily newspaper writing. I was suited to write in different forms. But I have continued to love newspaper folk and the wide and democratic reach of newspapers. I cherish my indoctrination into that world at a moment in my life when I could learn so much from it: how to write clearly and quickly; how to distill information; how to choose apt details; how to work within form but convey a distinct voice; how to go out into the city and simply talk to people and listen for their idioms; how to move outside of myself.

I left my brief stint in full-time journalism and enrolled in a one-year master's program in creative writing at Boston University. I was admitted into the fiction program but found my true vocation in study with Derek Walcott, whose poems I revered. At the end of that year I was absolutely clear that I wanted to be a poet, and I decided that a Ph.D. in English would prepare me for a career that could make sense and make possible my life as a poet. I also wanted to resume the enriching study of my undergraduate education, despite having proclaimed upon graduation—a scant year before!—that I was never going back to school, never writing another paper, never taking another test, never. During graduate school I continued to freelance as a journalist, mostly for the *Village Voice Literary Supplement* while that paper was in a truly golden era in black cultural criticism, publishing the work of (among others) Thulani Davis, Michelle Wallace, Greg Tate, Lisa Jones, Lisa Kennedy, Joe Wood, and Colson Whitehead.

Those were interesting times in the academy. African-American literature, which would become my field of expertise, was burgeoning. Literary theory was also in full effect; one graduate-school professor became incensed whenever a student spoke of "theory" instead of the teacher's preferred "criticism." The pieces in this collection mark years of fascinating and dramatic change in which the very definition of literature has transformed. To choose one example, when I first studied African-American literature, Zora Neale Hurston's *Their Eyes Were Watching God* was a cult favorite emerging from obscurity and back into print. Just thirty years later there are full-length critical studies of Hurston, dissertations, a Hurston Society, and biography and collected letters in print with major publishers. I've felt lucky to have a front-row seat to developments in African-American and feminist studies since the early eighties.

Reading as a woman. Towards a Black Feminist criticism. Gyno-texts. Aframerican theory. These were some of the terms and titles that were in the air when I began graduate study, and they opened my mind to the many ways that who we are affects how and what we read and think. The next important step of theorizing identity politics for me was to challenge monolithic assumptions of who "we" are; I am grateful that my leanings toward romantic or nostalgic group identities have been challenged. Yet still, I believe that great art shifts human beings, and that the widely defined culture of African-Americans will merit critical attention long after I'm gone. As I wrote in "Today's News," "we are not one, not ten, not ten thousand things / not one poem. We could count ourselves forever / and never agree on the number." I assume I have always "read as a poet," which is to say, there are various shapes of poetic argument and logic that no doubt inform how I recognize and craft argument in prose. Reading as an African-American woman intellectual poet? Reading, as my lodestar Audre Lorde would have it, with all of my selves active and present and vigilant and alive. The great utility of so much black feminist theory was the guiding truism that black women have blazed alternative routes to making sense of the world, that regardless of our differing circumstances, we have had to look from the outside to make sense of a world that has not endeavored to include us among its intellectuals.

The composition of the first section of this book, "Black Arts 101," emerges from my teaching years, which are ongoing. The first "black arts" class I ever took, "Problems in the Study of Afro-American Literature," featured a syllabus typed in a minute font on extra-long paper that covered three hundred years of the literature in all genres. Such was the field in 1982. Now enough progress has been made that African-Americanists can come out of graduate school without the obligation to be able to teach every single literary word ever written by an African-American, along with a full-fledged field of "white literature," as was still true as I was being trained. Now single-author seminars on writers such as Ellison and Morrison are de rigueur in many English departments. This section of the book can be thought of as one syllabus among thousands, a syllabus in which the "text" might be a novel or poem or painting or dance and in which that text might be examined by close reading, historical contextualization, or any number of other methods combined, as the guiding light of cultural studies has shown us.

While this entire book is evidence of one particular "Black Feminist Thinking," that section attempts to mark some of the aspects of my movement through years in which the term *black feminist* both took hold, was revised, and has ultimately been destabilized by the retrograde political forces we live with today. I hold on to the term both as it reflects my times and as it aptly describes some aspects of my mission.

Finally, and simply, I have always loved interviews with writers, and I want the final section to remind us how much thinking, theorizing, and history happens in talk, and how we must hold on to our galvanizing talking and what it memorializes.

My late grandmother, Wenonah Bond Logan, is often by my side when I am writing. Needless to say, she grew up during racial segregation in a world of sharply limited opportunities for black women. Yet she apparently possessed not one iota of gender or racial self-doubt. And though she never would have put it this way (because she was beguilingly taciturn and disapproved of excess in all forms), she loved what she came from: an incomparably rich community of black men and women who taught her all they knew and perfected the art of cherishing without coddling, ever. Only a fool would wish to be coddled.

When my grandmother finished college in 1931, she wrote to

a university in Denmark and said, "I imagine you have never had a colored student. I would like to be your first," and soon she set sail for the Continent. She had read "The Little Mermaid" and heard of her statue in Copenhagen harbor, which was unveiled in 1913. She wanted to see it. I do not know what it meant to her, but I do know that it gave her an idea that moved her geographically, emotionally, and spiritually beyond anything she had known to that point, and anything that anyone around her had imagined.

To go forth in my grandmother's questing spirit and explore the world of words and the ideas, power, and possibility they contain is what I have tried to do. I have tried less successfully to be as elegantly, fiercely understated as was she, but perhaps my voice and style are better suited to this century.

—Elizabeth Alexander
New Haven, Connecticut
January 2007

I

Black Arts 101

Dunbar Lives!

In the course of writing this essay I have found something that surprised me: Dunbar matters very much to contemporary African-American poets. And I have also discovered how Dunbar matters to me. Several years ago, in conversation with another African-American poet, I mentioned that when I was growing up my father would occasionally recite Paul Laurence Dunbar's "The Party." He did so joyfully and apropos of nothing but exuberance, as far as my brother and I could tell: "Dey had a great big party down to Tom's de othah night / Was I there? You bet. I nevah in my life see such a sight. / All de folks f'om fou' plantations was invited, an' dey come, / Dey come troopin' thick ez chillum when dey hyeahs a fife an' drum."

This was always a thrill. He had "slipped into the vernacular," as we said, vernacular always having the article *the* and one's movement from another kind of speech to said vernacular always described as "slipping." I think, actually, that noticing and loving these shifts in diction are what made me a poet, growing up around my mother's Sugar Hill Harlem queen's English; my grandfather's Jamaican music and vocabulary, use of figurative language; my grandmother's soft, drawn-out Alabama vowels mixed with etymological wizardry and syntactic starch shaped by her teachers in the 1920s at Paul Laurence Dunbar High School in Washington, D.C.; my father's magnificent Harlem vernacular; the Yiddish inflections and improvisational suffixing and wry humor of my parents' Jewish New York City schoolteachers; and then, oh how can I forget, the fluent Cackalacka spoken on the streets and front stoops of Washington, D.C., where I was reared in its eternal springtime. How could I not become a poet in the midst of all that cross-pollinating American

English? I should be a much better poet, actually, with all of that to draw upon.

But during this conversation with my black poet friend, she replied, "My father used to recite 'The Party' too!" This was surprising to both of us; I had thought of my father's recitation as being unique to our family, part of your own particular orality, our family syllabus. But the coincidence with the other poet gave me a sense of Dunbar as a poet whose legacy was intimately related to black home space and oral practice.

Certainly, if you asked a handful of contemporary black poets to quickly name who has influenced their work in the canon, you would be more likely I am certain to hear Brooks, Hayden, Hughes, and for younger writers, Sanchez, Baraka, Clifton, Dove, and Komunyakaa, named before Dunbar. Yet I suspect Dunbar resides in the gray matter of many black poets, the sub rosa given that crucially undergirds much of our practice regardless of background, training, region, and aesthetic. For, really, the century and the tradition are in some ways very short. Langston Hughes and Gwendolyn Brooks leapfrog the entire twentieth century for us if you think of how Brooks was personally known and in our midst for my generation of poets, and her long correspondence with Hughes as well as her early correspondence with James Weldon Johnson takes us directly to Dunbar himself. In other words, a Dunbar is only a great-grandfather to today's practicing poets. Though it was a busy century for African-American poetry and African-American people, nonetheless we are not far from what some might see as the significant beginnings of our traditions, the first black poet to do it "as a job," if you will, the very idea of the black poet, with attendant issues and contradictions in the life lived and in the aesthetics that remain relevant for us today.

I never studied Dunbar in school, not high school or undergraduate nor graduate school, even in African-American literature classes. African-American studies in the 1980s, when I was educated, had other business to attend to, mostly black women's literature (represented by the novel), the complex and thorny questions of criticism and theory, and literary resurrection and historiography. There just wasn't time for Dunbar, who I think, to be honest, might also have seemed a little old-fashioned, his majors and minors dichotomy set in stone.

My father's recitation of Dunbar was for pleasure, not for the purpose of creating another Negro poet. For me, there was something about his move into a vernacular poem that exposed me to and preserved—for the poem is fixed and not evolving language, even as its interpretations are fluid—something that either might not last or might not otherwise be known to his children that also connected him back to his mother and her parents. Why did he quote it to us? Was it to keep alive, if not specifically dialect, perhaps a holistic black world in an era of fevered integration? Despite the reference to plantations in the first line, I don't think my father thought of it as a slavery poem but rather as a "black space" poem that connected him, and thus, me, to the linguistic black communal speech that he grew up with that was not my experience as part of an integrating generation. When I asked him how he came to know the poem, he remembered the Countee Cullen anthology *Caroling Dusk* as one of his mother's favorites, and he believed he found the poem there, though "The Party" is not found in that volume, so the mystery continues. "Countee Cullen lived in the neighborhood, you know," he told me, activating my already hyperactive Harlem-as-Valhalla, born-after-my-time nostalgia. Then he told me, "The Party" was also a poem that many of his Harlem friends knew. In his group of boys, he said, you know that "if you recited it, someone would join in with you." Mind you, this was sometimes taking place in front of a building at 149st and Convent Avenue called the Paul Laurence Dunbar Apartments. But the young men didn't necessarily connect what they were saying to where they were saying it. They were woofing, being black together, marking black space with this poem.

In his 1991 introduction to his classic study *From Behind the Veil*, Robert Stepto coins the useful phrase "family bookshelf Afro-Americanists" to describe scholars of his generation who could say, "The first Afro-American literature course I took was the first one I taught." He is not only describing autodidacticism but more precisely a passing on of literary tradition that occurs within a black family or nonschool community context.

Scholars are beginning to loosen the knot between the fixed poles of Dunbar's "literary" and "vernacular." Dunbar was not so dichotomous. Yes, the "dialect" poets are obviously so, but even to name them effaces their sense of versification, of organization in verse, at the expense of their diction. They are not transcription. They are closer to English verse than they are to speech. When you look at the dialect and the standard poems side by side, their sense of verse, line, and meter is not at all dissimilar. And I would argue that as Dunbar's dialect poems are shaped by literary sensibilities, his literary poems are enlivened by vernacular energy and a rhythmic mastery that also emanates from that same source. The greatest of his standard verses are clearly not written out of a solely Anglo-American tradition. Perhaps that is Dunbar's genius, that high-low fusion that is also the greatest possibility of African-American poetry.

Back to "The Party." Think of the pleasure to be found there or in Sam Cooke's "Havin' A Party" or Luther Vandross's remake of same, with the "live" voices in the background echoing those more sinuous, sexy, breaking out of the sixties of Marvin Gaye's "Got to Give it Up," or even in "Madea's Family Reunion," which ends with a party on the very ground the slave ancestors ended up buying from their masters, the very cabin. In "Diary of a Mad Black Woman" as well there is a great big party held in the yard of the matriarch "Madea." Or think of Dave Chapelle's *Block Party*. The party scene is very important in black culture, and I think Dunbar's poem influenced it more than we know. Work is over. There is a vision of community here, and of an evanescent utopia. Displaced and dispersed families are reunited. For in Dunbar's poem the plantation context is at hand. "All de fouks from fou plantations was invited and dey come." They are called by "a fife and drum"; the slave community crosses plantation lines and assembles by wordless clarion call, echoed later in Baraka's more explicitly political call in "SOS": "calling all black people, black people come on in." They style, they fuss, they eat, and then they "dance dat suppah down," use the whole night because the day brings endless work and the brutalities of servitude that are not named in the space of the poem but haunt it because from the beginning we know we are in a plantation society. Dunbar is not eliding the horrors but rather preserving the space the slaves made for themselves. There are several instances in the poem where performance itself is embedded into the text. Dunbar is taking us as close as he can to the force and presence of those aspects of our culture that literary form will struggle to capture throughout the next century and also which is the powerful bedrock of black creative expression. In many volumes "The Party" comes right after "When Malindy Sings," another poem in which readers are invited to behold, hear, and witness the act of singing as part of the reading of the poem.

I realize only as I write this paper that I have written a poem called "The Party" which is a surreal, freaky-deaky grandchild to Dunbar's poem. The poem describes a party, a black block party in New York, and it opens "in the vernacular": "Obi had a big ole party." The speaker of the poem is dressed like Nefertiti; people drink rum and coconut water; Harry Belafonte appears; the party-goers dance to "an African band called Difunkt"; and the pregnant speaker's dress billows up around her, a flag of futurity and glorious possibility. The poem follows the exact same structure of Dunbar's "Party": declaration, then who came, what they wore, romantic drama, what they ate, how they danced, all in a joyous vernacular particular to time and place. In my poem appears a hydroponic baobab tree "whose roots explode into water"; the quintessentially African tree diasporizes within the poem in the way that Dunbar's poem can also be read as a story of diaspora and recombination in that he writes the slave community after it has in fact dispersed. The poems also have in common the wish to fix the beauty of black space and community. Consider here Dunbar's itinerancy, unusual for a black person of his time or frankly from anywhere, his movement from Ohio, Washington, Chicago, New York, England, all the time spent on the road to make his way as a black poet. My poem ends "rock on, rock on, rock on," which I think is meant to propel the utopic space into permanence, enduringness, eternalness, though it is evanescent. The stanzaic structure of Dunbar's poem is like a film strip; its narrative unfolds episodically, even cinematically. I suppose then what is interesting is that it literally never occurred to me that I was writing after Dunbar, but of course I was, and that is what is fascinating about influence, how it ferments sub rosa and comes up so that even the artist does not know she has borrowed, stolen, revised, paid homage.

I could explore at length the influence of Dunbar not just on contemporary African-American poetry but on African-American culture. Think of Abbey Lincoln's deconstruction of "When Malindy Sings." Or in film, for example, Zeinabu Irene Davis made her first feature, the ninety-minute *Compensation* in 1999, inspired by the brief Dunbar poem of the same name. The film is set in Dunbar's time. Davis uses silent film techniques such as title cards and vintage photographs to tell the stories of two love affairs between deaf women and hearing men. The film was made explicitly to be accessible to deaf and hearing viewers alike. How interesting that this short poem of a particular moment should move this very contemporary filmmaker narratively to the past but technically forward to innovation.

In the television film *The Rosa Parks Story,* directed by Julie Dash, we see a scene where young Rosa first meets Raymond Parks on a rainy day in the barbershop where he works. He is shaving a man and reciting "We Wear the Mask." The recitation is overlaid with a shot of a newspaper describing the woes of the Scottsboro boys, and one of the patrons in the shop cuts off the poem as though to dismiss its relevance to the more pressing social questions of the day. Poetry, and Dunbar, are for a moment put to the side of relevance. But don't forget that straight razor: The poem is reprised and finished when the white owner of the shop comes in and the men move their conversation about the Scottsboro boys into code speak. We later learn that Raymond Parks is helping the Scottsboro cause at great personal risk. He finishes reciting "We Wear the Mask" in the presence of the white boss in a powerful moment of signification. He has pulled one over on old Massa; not only has he hidden the fact of the black men's identification with and abettance of the Scottsboro boys, the scene also implies that the white man cannot understand or decode the Dunbar poem not only at the level of its signifying but also at the level of its elegant formal diction. This is to say, signifying does not always take place in the vernacular.

I wanted to know more about Dunbar's influence today, so I wrote and called an unscientific sample of black poets, and I sent out my query to the list-serve for the Cave Canem poetry community, which celebrated its tenth anniversary in 2006. The community of poets who have attended both the summer workshop and the regional workshops is over five hundred. Kalamu's ya Salaam e-drum would have been another cyber-place to have found probably more black poets at a sitting, and it might have been interesting to see if more of a southern aesthetic and sensibility arose from polling those poets. But for the purposes of this short paper, I thought a community of over five hundred known to me made sense as a starting place. I asked a few very simple questions: In what context did you first come across Dunbar's work, Which Dunbar poem first comes to mind for you, If you are a teacher, do you teach Dunbar, What do you think is Dunbar's ongoing significance to poets, and What have you learned from Dunbar?

I was struck by the force of people's responses and the overall sense that for black poets regardless of any number of different factors, Dunbar mattered. Poets wrote back swiftly and forcefully of "their" Dunbar. People thanked me effusively for giving them the opportunity to think about Dunbar. Those of a more experimental vein saw Dunbar as someone to play with, to riff on, to deform. Formalists were in awe of his capacities, consistently sounding the note that his fluency and mastery as a formalist had been underestimated. Many people had a very keen sense of his career, his struggles with class and color, his tragic early death, his violence toward his wife. In that regard he was a kind of celebrity for many black poets. He was "ours," so we knew the details of his life as well as his work. No one told me they learned Dunbar from a white teacher or in a predominately white school. He was either learned in a black school, from a black choir director or drama teacher outside of school, or at home. Many poets talked about the formal challenges of dialect, that writing dialect is not at all easy. Over and over they said that he was often learned orally; there were many poets who, like me, never saw Dunbar on the page until long after we knew his poems. But there were, also, many who talked about having a book of Dunbar in the house. Several poets mentioned a light bulb going off when they realized the title of Maya Angelou's book *I Know Why the Caged Bird Sings* came from a Dunbar poem as an important eureka moment of black intertextuality and literary lineage. One poet even said she had to fight in school with (black) classmates who claimed Maya Angelou made up the title herself!

Here are a few of the comments:

Lucille Clifton distinctly remembers her mother taking her on her lap, rocking, and reciting "The Party" and "Empathy." She recalled her mother as a great reciter and said that thus Dunbar "was a part of our own life. He became a part of my idea of what poetry was." She also said her mother told her that Clifton and Dunbar share a birthday, June 27, "and that was special to me." This calls to mind a similar maternal indoctrination into the tradition of black poetry, when young Gwendolyn Brooks's mother was known for introducing young Gwendolyn as "the Lady Paul Laurence Dunbar."

Reggie Flood: "My first experience of Dunbar was memorizing 'We Wear the Mask' for our African-American History week program. . . . My mother had me recite again and again those lines, not only to commit them to memory, but to learn how to 'become part of the poem' as she used to say. I remember that first moment years ago at the Formica kitchen table in Compton, my mom tapping out a steady rhythm to get me to respect the poem. In many ways it was my first real poetic experience."

Kevin Simmonds: "Believe it or not, when I was in high school [in a black neighborhood in New Orleans in the eighties] we would quote 'We Wear the Mask' when people were acting shady. Dunbar is quotable and reminds that poetry can be recalled in real time, in real life situations."

Herman Beavers: "What might Dunbar have become had he lived long enough to see the Harlem Renaissance? How would he have responded to modernism and the rejection of rhyme and meter by Eliot, Pound, etc.?"

Venus Thrash: "'We Wear the Mask' is so damned relevant to the black intelligentsia today, and that poem's meaning will always have significance in a world where we are still asked, overtly or covertly, to bend and bow in order to survive hopefully without breaking."

Forrest Hamer: "I first encountered Dunbar as an elementary school student in a segregated school in the south. We had 'chapel' every Friday. . . . Dunbar was a favorite choice of poets for us all, and the poems most frequently recited were 'We Wear the Mask' and 'Sympathy.' It interests me now that the poems recited in that setting tended not to include dialect."

Toni Asante Lightfoot: "It was 1976, I was 8 and Butterfly McQueen had just finished touring a show of Dunbar's work. Somehow my mother got her to perform at one of her fund-raiser parties for the Young Democrats. Ms. McQueen performed several pieces that night. However, the two that stick out the most for me now are her renditions of 'In the Morning' and 'Accountability.' I remember wondering why everyone laughed that someone had stolen one of massa's chickens and my mother and her friends giving me a little history lesson right there.

"In one class I taught, From Harlem Renaissance to Hip-Hop, I snuck in the poem 'Jump Back, Honey, Jump Back' as a type of rap. . . . As poets we don't know what seeds we plant and how they will grow. We also forget that even the seed that doesn't grow nourishes the soil for other life. Case in point, Once in a prison workshop one of the inmates said his favorite was 'He Had His Dream.' Several of his classmates also took that one on as their favorite and by the end of the class a graffiti artist of the bunch had painted a sign with the final words of the poem:

"'He saw through every cloud a gleam— / He had his dream.' Simple lines that powerfully resonated with the inmates."

Traci Dent: "[Dunbar is] where poetry begins for my grandparents' generation. It was Dunbar they recited at school and at local events. It was Dunbar's words they spoke with their Sunday scripture voices. Memorizing his work made them feel educated and proud."

Treasure Williams: "It is a secret wish that these things could only be for *us,* and the knowledge that they are too beautiful to be kept, so they must be shared and inevitably misunderstood."

Kendra Hamilton, in response to the question, "Are there any other questions that you think are important to ask about Dunbar's legacy?": "Yeah, we need to ask why he doesn't have more of one. Though his work was in a conservative form, and though he mined the vein of plantation nostalgia, his approach was very sophisticated—not at all the simplistic pap that his peers, white and black, were peddling. And his novel was one of the very earliest migration narratives, with the exception that his country mice came to grief in the big city and came back home. It's been years but I recall the ending being harrowing—the former slave returning to the plantation where the former master, mad and locked in an attic, howls like an animal when the sun goes down. . . . That sounds pretty modernist to me."

Kwame Dawes: "Color is no small matter with him. When you think about it, Dunbar was perhaps one of the first prominent dark-skinned writers to emerge at a time when African-American life was dominated and driven by lighter-skinned individuals from Booker T, to James Weldon Johnson, Frederick Douglass, DuBois and numerous others. Dunbar was in Jack Johnson's world in many strange and fascinating ways. He was dark, quite dark, and felt complicated by this blackness. He resented it and yet he understood it to be at the core of him. He was cut through with a strained sense of inferiority in the face of the 'purer' beauty of his wife. Self-deprecation is a mild term to use to describe his tone about his blackness. So that is his prison. This man who struggles to make things happen for him and yet manages to achieve so much—this man whose understanding of who his father was, whose understanding of heroism as a falsehood, who is part of the strange dilemma of wandering that haunted so many blacks after the war, is thrown into a world of fame and popularity that he could never understand. Dunbar was American to the core—a product of the American Dream with all its betrayals and lofty pretentions, and with all its remarkable capacity to make people believe they can achieve anything even when everything points the other way. I see him in that regard. I see him as tragic and sad. I see his violence to his wife, his violence to himself and his strange relationship to his mother as fascinating things. I see the way his 'friends' grew weary of him, started to see him as a man letting 'his blackness take over,' which we hear in much of the tone of letters by folks like J. W. Johnson and others who were concerned for him. Yes, race is critical to Dunbar, but not race as in black or white, but as if brown and black. Internal race dynamics. Few write about these things, but Dunbar makes us have to tackle that, at least a little bit."

Honoree Jeffers: "One thing you need to know is, I LOVE me some Dunbar. I am, after all, a black southern poet. Right now, when we are experiencing serious upheaval and population (as well as cultural) movement in the Deep South, I view him as an archivist of southern and migration culture. I realize he is not 'truly' southern, but he does represent the numbers of blacks who migrated from the South, so for me, he codifies black southern cultural expression. . . . As a middle-class African-American who has ancestral origins in the working class (and what black person doesn't?), my biggest question is how have issues of class and overt 'politics' in black poetics worked to exclude Dunbar from serious consideration? Why is Hughes viewed by many as 'the cut-off' for vernacular expression? In the black poetry community, are we still using DuBoisian standards for 'art and propaganda' to dismiss Dunbar? These are some of the questions I ask when I consider Dunbar."

Dante Micheaux: "Has he been silenced by a post-black poetic movement?"

Brian Gilmore: "A poet can be a star and a spokesperson for his people (his race). What made him so cruel to his wife, or what haunted him to be so destructive in the end?"

So you can see that from a moment in my childhood that reached back across a century, we have come to a place that is only a beginning: the consideration of the ongoing legacy of Paul Laurence Dunbar to African-American poetry.

(2006)

Sterling Brown

Where Academic Meets Vernacular

"Didn't you used to play ball with a dude called 'Spoons'?" the man in the market asked my father the other day. "Heavy-set fella, drove a red Jaguar?" That brief encounter in Washington, D.C., came back to me as I read Sterling Brown's poems for the millionth wonderful time. There is much to say about Brown's work, but what most characterizes his poems is the evident, utter joy the poet takes in listening to and reproducing black men telling tales, tall and otherwise. In his long life he understood that people speak gems every day, and he took it upon himself, in both his poetry and his critical writing, to gather, polish, and protect those precious turns of phrase. Chaucer and Shakespeare brought similarly vernacular energy to their pages in their times; perhaps that's a poet's best trick. Brown understood both the resonances and discontinuities of tradition and how he fit into that picture. I love it that "Heavy-set fella, drove a red Jaguar" just happens to be a perfect line of syllabic pentameter. Invocation of the once and future "Spoons" piques my fascination with the infinitely innovative tradition of naming and nicknaming found throughout the African Diaspora: even Walter Sisulu was called "Encyclopedia" in jail. My D.C. story made me picture Brown in some afterlife, holding court with a council of Slims, Smileys, and Big Boys.

Brown's first volume of poetry, *Southern Road,* was published in 1932. After that, though he published in periodicals, he did not have another volume until Broadside Press brought out *The Last Ride of Wild Bill* in 1975. Harper & Row first published *The Collected Poems* in 1980, as part of the National Poetry Series.

The idea of literary progeny and resurrecters in African-

American letters is an important one. To a people forging a literary tradition against the historical backdrop of withheld literacy and legal semipersonhood, questions of how black writers and other culture workers construct our literary heritage are relevant indeed. Brown's poems are frequently poetic versions of folktales that he casts in his particular seamless blend of the so-called folk and the so-called literary. In a sense he collapses the irrelevant distinctions between the two, calling simultaneously on the myriad voices in his tradition.

Brown has had as much of a role in the institutional construction of the African-American literary tradition as he has contributed to it as a poet. He was born in Washington, D.C., in 1901. In 1929 he settled into a fifty-year teaching career at Howard University. He supported black literature as "Editor on Negro Affairs" for the Federal Writers' Project; as codirector (with Ulysses Lee and Arthur P. Davis) of the abundant and trailblazing anthology *The Negro Caravan* (1941); as the author of his own literary scholarship, which examined images of blacks as well as black writing and folk culture. But no pulpit gave Brown more exposure than the teacher's, both at the university and, as legions of stories attest, at his Washington home. Hollie West reported in 1969 that a visitor to Brown's home was "as likely to find him playing host to Leadbelly as Ralph Bunche."

Brown casts his tales in various forms (ballads, blues, sonnets) and in the varying voices (monologues, dialogues) of his cast of characters. "Parish Doctor" shows the wary symbiosis between the doctor's knowledge and the knowledge of the community members he treats:

> They resent examinations,
> investigation
> They tell him what is wrong with them
> They know.
> It is pus on de heart, hole in de head
> The maul is open, they got
> stummatache,
> Somebody let some night air in the
> battens.
> They want him only to subscribe,
> The medcins: bitter-bitter is the best

> "Docteur, I doan b'leeve you can do
>   nottin fuh me.
>
> I got a snake in me. I know, me, I been
>   spelled."

Brown moves easily between voices in the poem both in the words he chooses and the spoken rhythms of the lines. The line "bitter-bitter is the best" jabs as doctor and patient, time and tradition, push up against each other.

Brown's poetic humor is crackling and legendary. "The New Congo," his send-up of Vachel Lindsay's "The Congo," "With no apologies," lampoons all that cult-of-the-exotica "Boomlay, boomlay, boomlay, boom." Brown plays on Lindsay's refrain, "Mumbo-Jumbo will hoo-doo you," ending his version with the mock prophecy, "Your Mumbo-Jumbo will get away from you. / Your Bimbo-Sambo will revolt from you."

I remember reading Lindsay's poem in high school and feeling terribly uncomfortable that I could explain neither my attraction to the language of the poem—it seemed, at least, *energized* to me then—nor my acute embarrassment at reading it from an anthology that had no black poets in a classroom full of white students with a white teacher. In a 1969 interview Brown commented on how it can be valuable to study work that has been called racist. "There's been so much trash written about the American Negro, and I think very frequently from what I read of the angriest of the [black] people, they dismiss all the literature of the past when they run across certain things that are said, not realizing there are many answers to their questions in this literature." Brown's poetry is unafraid of confronting stereotypes and putting a twist to them, and it is frequently through wicked humor that he takes apart cultural myths.

He also fortifies myths that he cherishes, like those of the "strong men" he venerates in his poem of the same name. In "Strange Legacies" Brown finds inspiration in the fighter Jack Johnson, and in John Henry:

> One thing you left with us, Jack
>   Johnson.
> One thing before they got you.

You used to stand there like a man,
Taking punishment
With a golden, spacious grin;
Confident.
Inviting big Jim Jeffries, who was
boring in:
"Heah ah is, big boy; yuh sees whah ise at.
Come on in . . ."

Thanks, Jack, for that.

John Henry, with your hammer;
John Henry, with your steel driver's pride
You taught us that a man could go
        down like a man,
Sticking to your hammer till you died.
Sticking to your hammer till you died.

Brother,
When, beneath the burning sun
The sweat poured down and the breath came thick,
And the loaded hammer swung like a ton
And the heart grew sick;
You had what we need now, John Henry.
Help us get it.

So if we go down
Have to go down
We go like you, brother,
"Nachal" men . . .

This poem is a gift outright; Brown is unabashed about heroes,
legacies, and what strengthens a community. "Strange Legacies"
is characteristic of Brown's work; his repetition and invocation
of the ballad structure, subtle rhyme that binds the poem, and
the exquisite sense of line-time that creates the weight and quiet
spaces in "Thanks, Jack, for that" and "Help us get it."

In his finest moments, Brown works a line's lyricism like no
one else. The idyll "Harlem Happiness" describes two lovers at
night: "We tasted grapes and tasted lips, and laughed at sleepy
Harlem. . . . / And then I madly quoted lyrics from old kindred
master, / Who wrote of you, unknowing you, for far more lucky
me— / And you sang broken bits of song, and we both slept in

snatches, / And so the night sped on too swift, with grapes, and words and kisses, / And numberless cigarette ends glowing in the darkness . . ."

There is, of course, more and more and more. In the absence of infinite time, I give you Brown's Hit Parade: "To Sallie, Walking": "Your vividness grants color where / Great need is, in this dingy town, / As you in pride of rose and brown / Threat the dull thoroughfare." "Strong Men": "*One thing they cannot prohibit—* / The strong men . . . coming on." "Ma Rainey": "I talked to a fellow, an' the fellow say, / 'She jes' catch hold of us, somekindaway.'" "After Winter": "*Butter beans fo' Clara / Sugar corn fo' Grace! An' fo' de little feller! Runnin space . . .*" "Pardners": "Wife was a thin spry corkscrew woman / With a tongue lak a rusty awl."

A flourishing African-American public presence is dependent on—among many factors—the notion of our resisting monikers, like "greatest," that encourage the notion that America can only think about one Negro at a time. That's why I resist calling Brown "the greatest!" this or that. I prefer to consider the particularities of his spot in the galaxy, which we know has an uncountable number of stars.

Of course, to be called "the greatest" is different when you're the one calling your own self great. That's "in the tradition" in a mode that Brown would relish, a tradition that includes Bessie Smith, Adam Clayton Powell, Muhammad Ali, Jesse Jackson, MC Lyte, and Slim Greer in the barbershop: "I kin talk out dis worl' / As you folks all know, / An' I'm good wid de women, / Dey'll tell you so."

(1990)

Nerudiana

When I was in third grade we were given the choice of learning Spanish or French. Most of the children chose French. To them it symbolized refinement, high culture, what a young person should know. I chose Spanish. I lived in Washington, which had residents from all over the world, and already I had a sense that for me, *Las Americas* was where it was at, that if I spoke Spanish, even *un poquito,* it would take me to people and places I wanted to be part of. I think it was clear to me that there was a world of "brown" people beyond brown Washington, D.C., and that world was calling.

As the years passed in school we learned to recite our obligatory Gustavo Adolfo Bécquer and the like. But Neruda was my first real Spanish language poet, from the seemingly "browner" world of Latin America, the first poet who showed me a way into both the self and the national, cultural self. I came to him as a teenager, so of course I came to him through love poems, which flung me wide open with their extravagance. "Quiero hacer contigo lo que la primavera hace con los cerezos" was the line of lines; love lived in metaphor; the body could explode like the miracle of spring. "Puedo escribir los versos más tristes esta noche." Why did I sometimes feel so tremulously sad, and why did the desire to write seem an inevitable and productive response? *Quiero,* that most wonderful of Spanish verbs, both "I want" and "I love," was an introduction to simultaneity and multiplicity of more than one thought and feelings, Whitman's multitudes contained within, or DuBois's two-ness. The genius Neruda who wrote those poems as a very young man wrote poems that somehow transcended the effulgence of late adolescence and its intense, transient, emotions.

I looked at my notes in my battered *Antologia Esencial* to get a sense of who I was at seventeen vis-à-vis Neruda. "NO PUEDO SEPARAR SU POESÍA DE SU VIDA," I wrote in big red letters, which I would come to understand as I later made my adult life. "Matilde es su primavera." "LIVING IN PLACE," again, in big red letters, made me think about the history of one's place and the impulse to speak for those whose voices have been muted. Neruda's exuberant catalogs were thrilling. He is poet of *y* ("el aire y el pan y la esperanza"), essentially inclusive but still discerning. And of course, those *odas*. How and of what do we sing? Interestingly enough, in my high school we were not taught only early, love lyric, pre–Spanish Civil War Neruda. We were taught a Neruda who sang of *las agonias de los Indios* and named the sins of Nixon and the United Fruit Company in his poems. "Pátria sin harapos," I underlined. I like the word *pátria* better than its cousin *patriotic*. It makes me feel that within the concept the word marks, there it is something deeper, loamier, fleshier, truer, wider, more hopeful.

June Jordan wrote: "I too am a descendant of Walt Whitman. And I am not by myself struggling to tell the truth about this history of so much land and so much blood, of so much that should be sacred and so much that has been desecrated and annihilated boastfully." I came for the first time to Chile to celebrate Neruda's hundredth birthday. Landing in Santiago, that last, breathtaking half-hour over the uninhabited Andes, all that land, all that sea, a specific place, its people, begin to exist for me beyond what I have read. *Inmenso* and *Vastedad* are two Nerudian words I relished, perhaps because, as someone who grew up happily in the urban confines of the East Coast U.S., spatial *vastedad* was not something I experienced nor viscerally understood. But I sensed it, and Neruda was an introduction for me to the necessity of looking to undertold history as a poetic wellspring urgently bubbling. Later on, in graduate school, as I began to imagine a life for myself as a person of letters, I studied Neruda in his political mode, in the context of Chilean, South American, and world politics. What could the poem say to the village or the world? Here was an example of a poet who was also a public man, and who seemed to wear those selves without conflict. How else to live in the world other than engaged with it? Why not use the poem to address wrongs, as well as celebrate?

I better understand now the compatible linkage of the political and the personal. I think about Neruda along with June Jordan, whose rageful work is also drenched in the light of love, a love that is often sexual, sensuous, and carnal. Jordan and Neruda engaged with what Martin Luther King called "beloved community," a community with which we struggle in love. Human beings move across these planes all the time.

The Nerudian lineage of New World poets includes many who are most important to me, reaching back to Whitman and forward to Gwendolyn Brooks, Kamau Brathwaite, and Derek Walcott, Yusef Komunyakaa's odes in *Talking Dirty to the Gods,* June Jordan everywhere, in love and in trouble, Sonia Sanchez and Robert Hayden in their epic "Middle Passages." But to come back to specific locale, Neruda helped me think: What is a Latin American poem? What is a voice of the Americas? Here with your public plazas I respond to the idea of the voice spoken in the town square, or love proclaimed, of ideology declared. Each country has its own version of a fraught political history—in my country it is the increasing "fast-food," disposable, cheap entertainment culture that has taken the place of productive politics, as well as an increasing, shameful refusal to understand anything about the rest of the world, narrowing the lens of our solipsism, fetishizing our September 11 without knowing that there are other September 11s, or that so many children a day die on the African continent from AIDS, calcifying the day so that children will grow up experiencing themselves as "us" and "them" feeling anxiously in need of reactionary patriarchal protection. This narrow worldview is an outgrowth of the way the country continually runs from really looking at its ongoing legacy of racism and discrimination emanating from the underacknowledged slave past. My country is also a place of certain freedoms, idealisms, and fresh starts, a place of dozens of inventive Englishes, a place of muchness, of *y,* as Whitman experienced and expressed it. Coming to Chile, and thinking anew about Neruda, helps me think about poetry and politics at home.

(2004)

Ode to Miss Gwendolyn Brooks
(*Ten Small Serenades*)

1. "A Lovely Love"

Think back to the first poems you loved. Perhaps those first-cherished poems spoke to a child's love of rhythm and rhyme, or put into words a sentimental truth that seemed profound when you encountered it but now seems matter-of-fact. What lasted? When I look back at my poetic passions, the one who has been with me all along is Gwendolyn Brooks. Her work resonates for me as much today as it did to me as a child thrilling to the urgent, bebop slang of "We Real Cool."

As the years have passed and I have myself become a working writer, I have been lucky enough to meet or hear many of the writers whose work has meant so much to me. Some have disappointed and others have exceeded expectations. Writers are, after all, just people who write, which is to say, they eat, sleep, love, work, wake up on the wrong and the right side of the bed, live in communities, and function like the rest of us, though their words tend to heighten our expectations of them. Gwendolyn Brooks is one writer whose artistic brilliance is matched by her humanity and generosity. Stories of this generosity are legion: young people whom she sent to Africa out of her own pocket; young people who have received awards from that same pocket. Her eyes are everywhere, and her endowments seem to come from out of the blue.

In 1997, I received a note from Miss Brooks announcing her awarding of the George Kent Prize to me—I was quite overcome, given that she is the poet I most admire. And when she sent me a personal check for my unexpectedly pricey plane ticket from the East Coast to Chicago, despite my protestations, because she wanted me to be able to come and collect the award, I became one of thousands who have been touched by this acknowledgment of good work and financial generosity. Miss Brooks is "an Encourager," she might write. With her many prizes she says, "You did a good job. Now keep going."

2. "Exhaust the little moment. Soon it dies"

She is queen of the specific, of titles that are themselves small stories, complete poems: "I love those little booths at Benvenutis"; "pygmies are pygmies still, though percht on Alps"; "The Sundays of Satin-Legs Smith"; "the white troops had their orders but the Negroes looked like men"; "The Chicago Defender Sends a Man to Little Rock"; "A Bronzeville mother loiters in Mississippi. Meanwhile, a Mississippi mother burns bacon."

3. "the mother"

What would American literature look like without her sleight of hand? For example, she chose the poet Michael Harper's first book, *Dear John, Dear Coltrane,* for publication in 1970. Imagine American poetry without that magnificent title poem, or "Brother John," or "Reuben, Reuben," to name just a few in that remarkable debut. "You were my clear winner," she wrote to him, a story he loves to tell. So many of us have similar stories to tell. Miss Brooks does her work quietly.

4. Brooks on Brooks

In 1994, the professor and writer Joanne Gabbin organized and hosted an unprecedented gathering of African-American poets at George Mason University. She called the conference "Furious

Flower" after Miss Brooks's great lines from "The Second Sermon on the Warpland," in honor of the lady herself: "The time / cracks into furious flower. Lifts its face / all unashamed. And sways with wicked grace." Professor Gabbin has edited the proceeding of the conference into an invaluable volume, *The Furious Flowering of African-American Poetry* (University Press of Virginia, 1999). It includes a wonderfully pointed interview with Miss Brooks. A few of her pronouncements: "I am an 'organic' Chicagoan." "The black experience is any experience that a black person has." "I want to report; I want to record. I go inside myself, bring out what I feel, put it on paper, look at it, pull out all of the cliches. I will work hard in that way." "I don't like the term African American. It is very excluding. I like to think of blacks as family. As a people, we are not of one accord on what we should be called. Some people say it doesn't matter, 'call me anything.' I think that is a pitiful decision."

5. Business

At the apex of her popularity, she left Harper and Row and took her work to black presses evermore. She put her money where her mouth was, shared the wealth, gave back, bought black.

6. Red Prairie

Bard of Chicago! Bard of the Southside: Bronzeville! Chicago and its Great Migrants, a literary imagination that sings not of Harlem but of Bronzeville. "The Last Quatrain of the Ballad of Emmett Till" closes: "Chaos in windy grays / through a red prairie"; the prairie where black migrants made Chicago. She gave the impeccable short lyric to the city, she went inside their homes, she wrought tableaux of their intimate lives, she venerated their intimate lives, she showed us the inside of a brown girl's head. She sings the song of the Southside of Chicago, that mighty city and its mighty black people.

7. Theme for English B (with apologies to Langston Hughes)

I. The Contributions of Gwendolyn Brooks to American Poetry
   A. A long and productive career spanning over 50 years, open to change.
   B. Unparalleled mastery of the urban ode.
   C. Syntactical genius. True to the quirky logic of innovative syntax. Fearless characterizer.
   D. No one is more economical with words.
II. Gwendolyn Brooks and the American Novel.
   A. *Maud Martha*! Formal innovations, a true poet's novel.
   B. How she faces intraracial issues of color, gender, class, unflinchingly. How ugly we can sometimes be, how jagged and hurtful to one another.

8. Blacks

She called her collected work *Blacks,* and what more is there to say, really? Pride in blackness is no insignificant matter. What does it mean to claim and celebrate blackness but remain complex and critical? "Blackness" she writes, "stern and blunt and beautiful, / organ-rich blackness telling a terrible story." She makes us think about what it is to be black, to struggle through blackness to struggle against and within one's community. She made her own struggle for racial self-acceptance public, in her autobiography, *Report from Part One.* And she showed us "the warpland" where the black soul resides, and in her sermonizing she told us to be both brave and compassionate. "Live and go out. /Define and /medicate the whirlwind."

9. Chaos Redux

How to write about the horror of racial violence? If you are Miss Brooks, you go within, go small, imagine the mad mind of the white woman who accused Emmett Till of impropriety, show us

the changed life she leads with her husband, the boy's mur-
derer, and then you will understand something about Emmett
Till beyond what his mutilated body said to the world. Hear Miss
Brooks inside Till's mother's head and feel the wind cut
through your ribs at the lines, "chaos in windy grays /through a
red prairie," and you will think about Amadou Diallo's mother,
and all the mothers, the mothers whom Miss Brooks under-
stands all too well.

10. Unfinished Tribute to Gwendolyn Brooks

(because imitation is the sincerest form of flattery)

Be righteous.
Radiate.
Worship nothing, honor everything.
Revere and protect what is small.
The universe is made of small things, of children.
Hear children.
Turn away from nothing. Face the sun.
Evolve at any cost.
Hoard nothing. Share.
Above all, be precise
so you may name the world precisely.
Let the heart and the guts lead the brain
and the big feet will follow.
Laugh loudly and often.
The heart is both fist and blossom,
opening and closing, closing, opening,
each time gathering new bounty.
Laugh loudly,
and often. Be righteous
and radiate.
Worship nothing, honor everything,
but today, let us venerate
Gwendolyn Brooks,
my first poet, our "First Poet."

(2000)

The Genius of Romare Bearden

It is difficult to imagine twentieth-century American art without Romare Bearden, and it is equally challenging to settle on a single topic when presented with the opportunity to write about his work. Do we choose a little-researched period in the artist's work, or in his life as a painter who was also a social worker, songwriter, traveler, intellectual? Or do we abandon scholarly methods and instead rhapsodize, exalt in the magnificent and meticulous scope of any given Bearden work? Do we think about the art in the context of New York City, Pittsburgh, Paris, St. Martin/St. Maarten, or Mecklenburg County, North Carolina? Do we focus on the medium of prints or consider also his early abstract oils? Dare we neglect the magnificent Bearden collage?

Grant Hill has wisely collected a dazzling group of Beardens that span the artist's career, from the early gouache paintings *Serenade* (1941) and *They That Are Delivered from the Noise of the Archers* (1942) to the great collages of the 1980s. Those early paintings give fascinating indications of what he achieves later on. We see his proclivities as the master colorist he fully becomes in the collage form; his interest in the (black) figure seen in geometric components; and, important Bearden icons such as the guitar. Viewers of this collection can begin to understand how a mature style develops by seeing these rarely seen early paintings. The 1979 collage in the collection "Time for the Bass" gives us Bearden in his exhaustive jazz mode. These works translate the energy, rhythm, and movement of jazz music into the flat form. This collection also shows us Bearden's urban and rural modes of Mecklenburg County and Harlem. Bearden's work displays great intimate understanding of those landscapes that outline the movement of so many black people from South to North in the Great Migration.

The Grant Hill Collection gives an opportunity to see not only the span of Bearden's career but also a generous selection of his collage work. For Bearden's work comes into its most mature form in collage, and it is not hyperbole to state that as a collagist he is without parallel. I want to focus on collage here first by discussing the work itself but then by thinking about how the Bearden collage gives us a way to think about the complexities of African-American identity. In that regard, we can look at Bearden as an important twentieth-century African-American theorist as well as one of its most magnificent visual artists.

Bearden refigured collage via European cubism, African-American quilting, and idioms of jazz and the blues. His subject matter has ranged from a retelling of *The Odyssey*, in vibrant blacks and blues, to scenes from the North Carolina of his early childhood. His iconography is magically commonplace: trains seen through doorways, roosters, doves, saxophones, trumpets, washtubs, clouds. Bearden moved through phases of abstract oils and cubist watercolors but found his fullest voice in the 1960s, when he began to work extensively in collage. His work combines any number of media, from newspaper and magazine pictures, to brightly colored paper, to fabric, watercolor, and thick black "Speedball" pens.

Everything you read and the stories people tell about Bearden say that he was a very clever man, analytical and dazzlingly well-read, humble without being self-effacing, respectful, and aware of himself in relationship to myriad traditions. While writing a paper about him in college, I decided I wanted to speak to him, found him in the New York City phone book, called him, and found him in, answering the phone, and willing to entertain my questions. By the end of the conversation he had sent me to Sun Tzu's *The Art of War*, any stained glass windows I could find, and Earl "Fatha" Hines's music, so that I might better understand his own work. Bearden had digested a wide range of influences to arrive at the specificity of his vision.

Here is a quotation from Bearden, on his own identity: "I think of myself first as an American, and being an American means four things. One, being in the tradition of Emerson, Emily Dickinson, Melville, Walt Whitman. Second, you have to have the spirit of the whole Negroid tradition. The third tradition is the frontiersman, like Mark Twain and Bret Harte, and the fourth tradition is the Indian."[1] W. E. B. DuBois wrote these lines in 1903, in *The Souls of Black Folk:* "One ever feels his two-ness,—an American, a Negro; two souls, two thoughts, two unreconciled strivings; two warring ideals in one dark body, whose dogged strength alone keeps it from being torn asunder."[2] "One ever feels his two-ness" would become a veritable mantra to legions of students of blackness and DuBois's image of an ineffably split African-American consciousness, and of bifurcation as the major twentieth-century trope for African-American consciousness, remains resonant today.

But over one hundred years later, the "two-ness" trope must be revised. If the African-American intellectual consciousness is split, it is split multiply rather than doubly, and that that so-called fragmentation, arisen from the fundamental fragmentation of the Middle Passage, has become a source of our creative power. The complex coexistence of a spectrum of black identities in a single space—think of Bearden's own self-description above for example—represents a particular strength and coherence of African-American cultural production. Formal conflict is the locus of true innovation such as that which is evident in the twentieth-century African-American tradition from *Souls* back to Anna Julia Cooper's *A Voice from the South* to *Cane* (Jean Toomer), to *Invisible Man* (Ralph Ellison), to *Mumbo Jumbo* (Ishmael Reed), to *The Bluest Eye* (Toni Morrison), among others. In order for DuBois to make a space for his "type" on the literary continuum, that type being the twentieth-century heretofore unimagined African-American intellectual who would write a book with the formal multiplicity and referentiality of *Souls*, he had to "make" a multiple self in the text at hand. In other words, the structural hybridity of the book *Souls* necessarily makes the written space in which he can fully explore aspects of what I would call his "collaged" identity. And collage, as developed and employed by Bearden, is my model to describe the presentation of self-identities in African-American literature and culture. Critics have used collage to talk about the literary works of modernist writers such as Joyce, Pound, and Eliot, as well as in Dadaist novels and various postmodern forms, but the Bearden collage offers a more necessarily historical—and culturally particular—

context for twentieth-century African-American literature and culture.

Collage lets us think about identity as a spoked wheel or gyroscope on which its aspects spin and recombine. Collage also allows us to see African-American creative production as cohesive rather than schizophrenic. In other words, the disparate aspects of personalities and of influence that might seem contradictory can actually coexist in a single personality, or a single identity. When the process of cutting and pasting is visually evident—as it is in the cut and torn edges within Bearden's collages—yet obscured—by the fact of the unified whole the picture represents—creative/constructive process itself is valorized as a crucial and *aesthetic* component of the path to artistic coherence, and, indeed, an avenue to understanding how "coherence" itself is evaluated.

Collage, in both the flat medium as well as more abstractly in book form and as a metaphor for the creative process, is a continual cutting, pasting, and quoting of received information, much like jazz music, like the contemporary tradition of rapping, and indeed like the process of reclaiming African-American history (or of any historiography). African-American culture from the Middle Passage forward is of course broadly characterized by fragmentation and reassemblage, sustaining what can be saved of history while making something new. Collage constructs wholes from fragments in a continual, referential dialogue between the seemingly disparate shards of various pasts and the current moment of the work itself, as well as the future the work might point toward. Ralph Ellison said, about Bearden:

> [Bearden] has sought here to reveal a world long hidden by the clichés of sociology and rendered cloudy by the distortions of newsprint and the false continuity imposed on our conception of Negro life by television and much documentary photography. Therefore, as he delighted us with the magic of design and teaches us the ambiguity of vision, Bearden insists that we see and that we see in depth and by the fresh light of the creative vision. Bearden knows that the true complexity of the slum dweller and the tenant farmer requires a release from the prison of our media-dulled percep-

tion and a reassembling in forms which would convey something of the depth and wonder of the Negro American's stubborn humanity.[3]

And here, a quotation from Picasso on collage: "If a piece of a newspaper can become a bottle, that gives us something to think about in connection with both newspapers and bottles, too. The displaced object has entered a universe for which it was not made and where it retains, in a measure, its strangeness. And this strangeness was what we wanted to make people think about because we were quite aware that our world was becoming very strange and not exactly reassuring."[4] Picasso's displaced "object" could be thought of as the African body, then the African-American body in migration, and collage as the process through which that "body" makes sense of itself in a hostile and unfamiliar environment.

Any discussion of the African-American collage must include a discussion of the quilt. Quilts embody the simultaneous continuity and chaos that characterize African-American history in all spheres. If African-American creativity is always in some way grappling with African-American history by trying to knit together the fragmentation that forms its core and the paradox of fragmentation as a center, quilting is a motif for a creative response to that history. Romare Bearden himself understands how quilting fits into African-American social, creative, and visual history. He has represented the act of quilting in his work, and his collages allude to strip weaving, quilts, and textiles. He also utilizes actual scraps of fabric. He has called his collage-making "precisely what the ladies (at the quilting bee) were doing."[5] The bits and pieces that make quilts as well as collages all refer to their uses and places in other lives; the life of the quilt is the aggregate of those pieces, and the work then becomes a referential discussion of both past and present at once.

West African, Mande-influenced strip weaving in which narrow strips of cloth, sometimes as many as one hundred, were sewn together to make larger pieces of cloth or garments, was a crucial precursor to the African-American quilt. The patterns that made their way into the African-American tradition were the so-called "crazy quilt" patterns, seemingly irregular contrasts of color and line. These West African fabrics were collaged in the sense of being disparate pieces put together, though they do not have the same system of diverse referents as New World collages; once these textile traditions reached the Americas, they arose of different material and historical circumstances, and the textile work, as with other arts and crafts, reflected those new circumstances. Still, the concept of the process of putting pieces together and the improvisational possibilities inherent in the different color and pattern contrasts relate to the concept of collage. Strip weaving and quilting are not the same as cutting a pattern for a dress, where each piece is predetermined and the end outcome of the whole can be anticipated. Rather, when strips of cloth are sewn together, like strips in a quilt, the creative process continues throughout that act, through the matching and setting of color to color and pattern to pattern.

Fon-influenced appliquéd textiles also found their way to the African-American quilting tradition. Those African textiles set up intricate symbolist landscapes and told stories, strongly derivative of Egyptian hieroglyphics. African-American story quilts, in particular Harriet Powers's story quilts, between 1886 and 1898, blend the New World necessity of sewing bed covering with Old World information about textile work, a New World manifestation of ancestral motifs and narrative impulses.[6]

An African-American quilt might be made from pieces of blanket wool, worn cotton from an apron, a soft piece of calico from a fourth-hand dress, made of the materials of the new place, but could nonetheless reflect the patterns of an ancestral heritage, just as slaves made instruments from whatever was at hand—washtubs, broom handles, even their own bodies in hambone and spoons. A washboard could make sounds and music but was also, or had been, an instrument of work, a historical referent of the condition of the creator. The object had its contemporary life and meaning as well as its ulterior "lives," all in the same site. If nothing else was available, when even the body was not legally one's own, the body nonetheless could become a site for creative assemblage.

Composite visual works are ancient and cross-cultural. In the twelfth century Japanese calligraphed poetry was made of cut and pasted pieces of delicate paper. Thirteenth-century Persian artists cut leather into flowers for bookbinding. In the early seventeenth century and quite probably earlier Mexican feather mosaic pictures were made, and in the same century in Europe mosaic pictures were made of such earthly objects as beetles and corn kernels. Eighteenth-century European collages were made from butterfly wings, and in midcentury the still-familiar British tradition of Valentines commenced. According to art historian Herta Wescher, there is "nothing very new about the essential idea of collage, of bringing into association unrelated images and objects to form a different expressive identity."[7] Eddie Wolfram observes, "Besides their functional reality, some mundane objects have always held the potential of an 'inner,' more magical reality that is connected with man's wonder about the nature of existence and his own destiny."[8]

Collage, per se, entered the art historical lexicon in the early pat of this century, as an outgrowth of cubism, and cubism, of course, developed as its practitioners were becoming familiar with and consequently inspired by different kinds of African art. Gregory Ulmer calls collage "the single most revolutionary formal innovation in artistic representation to occur in our century,"[9] and states that the innovation broke with traditional realism in its interplay between what Bearden called "mosaic-like joinings" and the unified image viewed from a greater distance. Wescher insists that twentieth-century collage was scarcely influenced by these earlier developments by "craftsmen, folk artists, and amateurs," folk and religious artists, which seems dubious, but certainly this was the first time that collage was employed by creative artists as the outgrowth of a specific artistic movement.

The word *collage* comes from the French *coller*, meaning to paste, stick, or glue. Claude Lévi-Strauss would play with that root when in *The Savage Mind* he used the term *bricoleur*, for he or she who made do with whatever was at hand, "with a set of tools and materials which is always finite and is also heterogeneous."[10] The first collages recognized as such were Pablo Picasso's *Still Life with Chair Caning* and Georges Braque's *Fruit Dish*, both made in 1912; there is some dispute over who made the first of what we now call collages, Picasso or Braque; both claimed credit, and Picasso may have predated *Still Life* to place himself first. But at this point of the cubist movement both artists had similar aims.

In cubism, painters attempted to show their subjects from as many sides or perspectives as possible at the same time. This concept revolutionized the world of possibilities in modern art by introducing the concept of simultaneity and a departure from the flat, literal surface. Collage juxtaposed seemingly disparate elements into a new context and a new whole. Braque said that in collage he could separate color from form, thus allowing both to "emerge in their own right" (Perloff, 24) or exist simultaneously together and apart.

The displaced "object" Picasso mentions in the above quotation is, in African-American terms, first and foremost the displaced African body. There is also a "displaced," or, to riff on Carter G. Woodson, "mis-placed," galaxy of cultural and historical references that the African-American cultural worker draws upon. Historical distortions are deliberate and not at all haphazard; we are displaced in that we were taken from Africa, and we are misplaced in that we have been put in a place, both literally and figuratively, that does not acknowledge the full complex dimensions of our existence. Culture workers must then continually strive to create, validate, and keep in circulation written evidence, traces, of actual cultural existence. The quilt or collage creates something new that is simultaneously what it was and what it might be, due to its referentiality. The finished product is always a reflected breakdown of selections, the mechanics of choosing. The act of making is inherent in the finished thing itself.

When Bearden cuts colored paper rather than representational newspaper and magazine images, the shapes he makes from the paper become repeated motifs, his ritual shapes and images that continually call attention to a depth and a life behind the canvas itself. Bearden has said:

> In most instances in creating a picture, I use many disparate elements to form either a figure, or part of a background. I build my faces, for example, from parts of African masks, animal eyes, marbles, mossy vegetation, [and corn]. . . . I then have my small original works enlarged so the mosaic-like join-

ings will not be so apparent, after which I finish the larger painting. I have found when some detail, such as a hand or eye, is taken out of its original context and is fractured and integrated into a different space and form configuration it acquires a plastic quality it did not have in the photograph. (Bearden, *A Memorial Exhibition*, 26)

Bearden first ventured into collage explicitly in 1951 with *Untitled Duke (Ellington) and Billy (Strayhorn)*,[11] and he experimented with Egyptian hieroglyphics in a "Hierographs" show in the forties as well as pointed shapes and a concern with black, line, and color that would recur in later collages.[12] It was not until the 1960s that he was fully involved in collage as his primary art form.[13] Hs watercolors in the forties and early fifties are frequently separated by heavy black lines; he was playing with the idea of blocks or patches of color that would resurface in the collages. But the crucial difference in collage is the concept of overlapping. Separated spaces and blocks of color do not represent an integration of disparate segments in the same way that overlap and consequent recombination underpins the very concept of collage, especially as I am using collage to talk about identity formation. I am arguing for an African-American identity that is not segmented but rather a curious whole. Collage becomes a way to remember—and the process of remembering and refiguring, whether literal or metaphorical, is inherent in the African-American literary critical enterprise—and find a vehicle in the act. A look at the process of piecing together in Bearden's work will provide a bridge to understanding the same process at work later in African-American written works.

Untitled: Duke and Billy, which appears to be the earliest of Bearden's published collages, is a whimsical postcard (the catalog lists size unknown). A dutiful Billy Strayhorn and a jaunty Duke Ellington stroll by a Paris book stand in a snapshot on the left side of the plane. On the right, Bearden has made ink line drawings of cliché Paris postcard scenes: the Eiffel Tower reaching to the clouds, a bridge over the Seine, a *jeune homme* in ankle-pants and striped sailor shirt. The background is green, and red, white, and blue stripes to suggest the French flag govern the frame in titled rectangles. "Duke and Billy" is handwritten in red and blue underneath the photograph. What makes this collage most interesting is that Bearden has pasted cut sections of photo contact sheets of Ellington and Strayhorn in what looks like a Parisian train station. The contact sheet both represents time in the collage—the sense of a whirlwind trip as exemplified in the rapid shifts between the frames—as well as an intimacy: Was Bearden there? Did he take the pictures? They are not posed portraits but rather snapshots; how did he come upon them? Bearden leaves off the last names of his subjects to suggest that either he is intimate with them or that we should be intimate with the subjects, "Duke" and "Billy" to all. The public France of the postcard moves quickly to the intimate France, and the larger cultural juxtaposition is one of these two black American musical greats bringing their black jazz to Europe. This minor collage illustrates how referentiality embedded in the objects juxtaposed on the page opens up the fields of meaning in the work itself.

In Bearden's collages, you see the simultaneous referentiality—the "past life" of the cut or torn fragment—as well as the contemporary moment or whole that these reintegrated fragments create. Bearden's 1971 collage *The Block I* is a long horizontal rectangle, setting up a sense of the forward movement of narrative from the start. Though Palmer Hayden and Archibald Motley are the artistic parents of the African-American street scene, Bearden was the first to go behind the facade of the black inside his subject's homes and lives. For the buildings he has used plain brown papers, bricks he has painted himself, and what looks to be brick-patterned Contac paper, reminiscent of the wood grain paper used by Picasso in those first collages. He has "cut" into the buildings not solely in the regular spaces where windows would be but rather at random spots, as though cutting through the brick. In this way the viewer feels less like a peeping Tom than like a privileged observer placed squarely in the middle of life lived. The irregularity of the cuts adds to the element of spontaneity and therefore "authenticity." Yet he also makes a viewer aware of this status of invasion, of looking in without having asked permission. Additionally, because we do not see into every room, the viewer is aware that choices have been made of what to reveal and what to keep private. The grave boy looking out might be asking, Who are you? as the viewer asks the same questions. The angels burst from the brick at the top of the work, making us aware of the constructed frame that defines and sometimes constricts a community as well as the spiritual necessity of imagining movement beyond those boundaries.

In the Grant Hill Collection, we see a similar scene in *The Street* (watercolor and collage on board, 1985). The sense of a public black life and the private life beyond is made clear. The haunting black faces cut out from other places find themselves at home on this street. Yet their eyes speak of elsewhere, referring again, perhaps, to the Great Migration that was part of Bearden's own experience and that he understood as emblematic to black people in this country as they have moved and reassembled from one country to another, one region to another, even one block to another, adapting and evolving with each geographic shift.

Bearden's interiors also give us a sense of the intimacy with which he knew and saw black life, and his use of collage adds dimension to that sense of intimacy. In *Morning Gingham* (1985) two women prepare for the day, one bathing and the other preparing water or food. They occupy the same space, faced in opposite directions, each performing her own ablutions, distinct yet together. The gingham in the collage is actual fabric that serves both to represent a woman's skirt and a window curtain, but also to allude to a culture where nothing is wasted, where materials are recycled, and where stories are embedded in objects or materials. The recent Whitney Museum exhibit "The Quilts of Gee's Bend" magnificently showcases women who work together intimately—so in a sense this is collective or communal work—but their individual voices and aesthetics are also blazingly clear. The so-called Negro spirituals came from a collective context and collective authorship, yet they made space for the solo voice to be heard, individuality out of community.

You don't have to believe in magic to believe that objects carry something from one person to another. Think of the old wedding tradition that a bride should wear something old, something new, something borrowed, and something blue. The "something borrowed" is meant to bring good luck and blessings to the bride from the person who first wore the brooch or carried the handkerchief. Few would dare break with such tradition. So it isn't a leap to understand that the bits of cloth that came from garments someone actually wore bring a bit of that person with them. To translate this to Bearden's artistic practice, as one imagines that many of these previous owners were unknown to him, he is bringing something of the actual spirits of black people into his work in a way that paint alone never could. In the Grant Hill Collection we see this especially in *Morning Charlotte* (1985) and *The Evening Guitar* (1987). For what is DuBois's double consciousness than the sense that we are scrutinized even as we make private space, that we are imagined even as we imagine ourselves? Bearden understood that paradox profoundly, and he managed the feat of making it visibly manifest in his collaged work. He also gave us a world of its own integrity, that could be spectated, if you will, at the same time that it enjoyed the free play of imagination and self-invention. Most importantly, it managed to convey profound intimacy. Bearden's genius is placed in context of a long and fruitful career in this collection.

(2003)

Lucille

There were many books in my home when I grew up. Few of them were books of poetry. I remember four, to be precise, and I remember them sharply, because I read them over and over again: A palm-sized, leather-bound Shakespeare's sonnets, Leroi Jones's *The Dead Lecturer,* Archibald MacLeish's *The Wild Old Wicked Man,* and Lucille Clifton's *Good Times.* Lucille Clifton's book opened,

> Here in the inner city
> Or, like we call it,
> Home.

"Here" we are, I read from Washington, D.C., here someplace that was "home," as "we" called it, beyond the reach of sociological language like "inner city." That "we" made me think of the "we's" my parents used when they meant more than those of us who were in the rooms. We black people, we city dwellers, we who ardently believed this or that, we our family and beyond our family. We. What did we agree was home?

As a child, I thought I understood those poems, and I did, but the miracle of Lucille Clifton's poems is how they turn and unfold, close and turn again, as you stay with them over the years. I held onto some passages like

> Children
> When they ask you
> Why is your mama so funny
> Tell them, she's a poet
> She ain't got no sense.

As my children grow, I am increasingly grateful for those lines.

I taught Lucille's poems on Tuesday to an exceptional group of students and I watched them also enact that turning, holding the small perfect things to the light, accepting the meditations they invite. We held Lucille's poems to the unsedimented light, the *luz,* the Lucille her poems tell us she was chosen to receive. My students reminded me, too, of the light she shows us in "Lucifer," "illuminate I could /and so /illuminate I did."

I think the richest lessons her poems have taught me are about the proximity of life to death, and the porosity between those realms. Lucille matter-of-factly communicates in poems with a grandchild before he is born, her husband, after he has died, her mother, after she has died. There is dreaming and waking, there is life, there is death, cancer is cancer, there is wellness and there is illness, but within those states there are many ways of knowing, listening, learning, perceiving. Her poems call upon all those modalities and recognize the flow between them. Every shut eye ain't sleep, every good-bye ain't gone. That's one of the many things Lucille Clifton's poems have shown me, and to trust what you know from the body, through the porous scrim between waking and dreams, this life and others.

When my first baby was ten weeks old and I was just beginning the long journey of figuring out how to be his mother, Lucille was the one, at a poet's retreat, who pried him from my arms and told me, simply, "You need to eat now." We are so lucky to have been graced by her grace, for every word she's written and for all, Lucille, that you are.

(2004)

Living in Americas

Poems by Victor Hernández Cruz

Página is the better word than *page:* the English word just sits there, while the Spanish moves like—well, like flipping pages. *Escribimientos* is rather cumbersome in contrast to its English cousin, *scribblings,* which looks, on the page, like what it is. *Guayaba* stays the same in either language (depending on how you speak it), but what does it mean to someone who has never seen the fruit's elemental curve, or tasted its pink?

These are the linguistic waters Victor Hernández Cruz navigates in *Red Beans,* a collection of poems and prose musings which marks his twenty-second year as a published writer. Random House brought out his first full volume, the Nuyorican classic *Snaps,* in 1969, when Cruz was nineteen years old and a self-described "teeny-bopper" from the Lower East Side. His published work since then includes *Mainland* (1973), *Tropicalization* (1976), and *By Lingual Wholes* (1982).

"Migration is the story of my body, it is the condition of this age," Cruz writes in the essay "The Bolero of the Red Translation," in the beginning of *Red Beans.* He is currently living *campesinamente* in Aguas Buenas, Puerto Rico, where he was born in 1949, a town "bombarded by . . . insectology of the strangest biologies and at night the sound of distant brewing." Cruz moved to New York at age five and then, as a young adult, to the Bay Area, where he lived until this last move. He remains, in his written words, "a body of migration, an entity of constant change."

Cruz writes in an English that incorporates—in the exact sense of the word—Spanish as well. The early argot of *Snaps* might be called "Spanglish" or "Nuyorican" (with a West Coast dollop). In a recent telephone interview from Aguas Buenas, Cruz called it "a combination of Puerto Rican slang and Black English, and then there's that Jewish lilt that everybody gets in New York." He is an acute observer of the Englishes of fellow writers like Conrad and Kosinski, languages bred in a world where "bilingualism is the norm rather than the exception."

Cruz insists that multilingualism has always been the state of the art for writers. "Look at Ezra Pound, he used 13 languages in the Cantos. He even had Chinese characters in there," Cruz says. "[U.S.] television always had the phrase, 'See you pronto.' If you name the mountains, and the valleys, and the rivers, and the towns in the Southwest, you're practically speaking Spanish, so I think Spanish is an integral part of the North American experience at a much larger level than people are admitting. My poetry is very North American in that sense."

Cruz's poetry over the years has always been clever and filled with word and sound play. He wields narrative at a storyteller's leisurely pace even as the poems snake down the page. The poems move with Cruz's migratory imagination from New York to Hawaii, San Francisco to Amsterdam. Puerto Rico is both real and imaginary, a place where things happen as well as a mythological motherland remembered. Cruz is knowledgeable about the history and culture of the creolized Caribbean and its pre-diaspora roots; he claims African, Indian, and Iberian kin by weaving music and legends throughout the poems. When one of his women wonders, "what is rice if it doesn't fluff," or reaches out the window for a letter, daily rituals snap into focus as culture fighting to perpetuate itself in different accents and on different turf. He draws people, places, customs, and history on the head of a pin, as in "El Club Tropical."

> . . . Pito
> Pito of the shiny green shirt   with
>   all his African Powers
> hanging from his neck . . .
> What time was it   was it time for
>   another day to be born to
> originate in the middle of quiet valleys
>   to come and eat us like

> moving fog   It was a warm night
>   when you dancing God can't
> be far.

The poems in *Red Beans* are lean, clean, and historical. In "Snaps of Immigration" he remembers his mother caressing parsley in the supermarket and new English "Like trumpets doing yakity yak." Many of the poems contemplate the color red, in roosters, red dirt, the Red Sea, red beans, of course, and "[t]he hidden / Red pepper / In a stew / Not the thing itself / But the shadow." The tight rhythms in Cruz's poems reflect his own listening, from doo-wop to *guaguanco* via "[m]arimba tango samba / Danza Mambo bolero / . . . Maraca guiro and drum / Quicharo maraca y tambor / Who we are / Printed in rhythm and song."

Though Cruz has published fiction and nonfiction prose before, *Red Beans* is the first of his books to contain so many essays. In our interview, he spoke about the difference he sees between poetry and prose. "If I bring a question up I feel I have to answer it in prose, whereas poetry is more suggestion. . . . The prose is like a map. I want to take them to a specific place and have them see a specific opinion I have." The most powerful essays in *Red Beans* emerge from between the "map" and the sound-conscious dreamworld of a poet who would "never put 'mango' next to 'technology.'"

The section entitled "Morning Rooster" contains prose odes to salsa music, Old San Juan, and *Mango Mambo*, Adal Maldonado's book of photographic portraits of Latin musicians. Cruz's passions are eclectic; he offers sober musings on the approaching five hundredth anniversary of Columbus's voyages to the Americas a few pages after narrating a poetry bout between himself and Andrei Codrescu in Taos, New Mexico. "The gladiator spirit exists in poetry at many levels, so why not focus it with a poetry reading bout?" Cruz asks. The two jousted before an audience of five hundred, some of whom bet cash on the outcome. A victorious Cruz riffs like his own Bundini Brown: "So gua-gua-gua. I say to my possible opponent next year she or he better bring rhythm, content and flavor, for I am sharpening the nails of my rooster, and I don't care where their content is from, for I am a Caribbean frog—and those jump every-which-way."

"The Bolero of the Red Translation" is a memoir of migration in which "[m]en with huge wavy pants and shoes like boats stood in clusters smoking cigarettes pointing towards the sky suggesting other dimensions." Once Cruz was in New York, where Spanish was forbidden in school and English "sounded like bla-bla-bla," culture still replicated itself in "story sessions in that grandiose manner known to all Latin Americans, el cuento campesino, phantasms arrived through coffee pots, pictures shook on walls and dead relatives peeled off."

"Bolero" then becomes a tract on poetry, an addition to a long line of *ars poeticas.* "Poetics is the art of stopping the world," he writes, "asking it the basic question: Where are you coming from? Putting a mirror in front of its big face, deciphering its emotional ingredients, speculating on its intent."

The "big face" of the world has long fascinated Cruz, even before he was a Lower East Side teenager mining Gotham for inspiration and adventure. "I come from the old New York, the old neighborhood New York," he told me. "I was able to get a classic New York upbringing—stickball, kick the can, the street life. You could walk in the streets, you could go get yourself a knish and bring it back to your house and put the knish next to your rice and beans. You could go to Avenue A and get yourself a pizza, and you knew the numbers people, and everything had its patterns." At sixteen he published his first chapbook, *Papo Got His Gun,* on a mimeograph machine used by the Eleventh Street Block Association to print rent strike leaflets, then sold it to bookstores around town for seventy-five cents a copy.

Cruz kept writing and fell in with a group of African-American writers that included Ishmael Reed, David Henderson, and Clarence Major. "Every time they'd start to publish, they'd say, what to do with Cruz? And I was of course young, and my sense of coming from a *criollo* culture, my sense of racial separation, would be different from an Anglo kid, so I said yeah, here's the poem." He published in the late lamented *Negro Digest* and *Umbra* as well as in magazines like *Progressive Labor* and *Evergreen Review.* "I'm a *criollo* person," he says, "in blood and culture."

Cruz is now at work on a new novel, *Time Zones,* which

emerges from his sense of change in different sites of migration. "The whole sense of change here [in Puerto Rico] is different. Some people are still into the boleros of the thirties and forties. Some people—they call them *roqueros*—they like metal rock. Some people like the salsa of the sixties, some people are at the turn of century. There's less uniformity. Here, there's the possibility that some people might be in the last century with those ideas and fears, a sense of life."

Puerto Rico has been the right place for him to explore those zones. The poetry he's writing is in Spanish—though, perhaps, a Spanish as hybrid as North American English. "I wanted to write in Spanish," he said, "which is full of Arabian words, it's full of African words, it's full of those rhythms and patterns, and when I write in Spanish, no matter what the poem is about it's full of history, because one word would remind me of the history of that word, not just the sound of the word, and the poem then becomes a crowd of stuff, of history and psychology and energies."

What would be treacle in the hands of lesser souls is quirky and utterly lovely in *Red Beans* and in Victor Cruz. His nostalgia is a way of remembering as well as an avenue of response to the present. "I remember," he says once again, "and I'm in another time zone, too, seeing *jíbaros* in the plaza with those hats. You know, there was a sense of hat on the island. You see the old pictures from the forties here of meetings and groups, and all the men had those straw hats and those *pra-pras*—you remember those flat-top hats? With the ribbon around them? This place was rampant with beautiful straw hats. You don't see that as much now, but I remember when I was a kid here, everybody had that sense of hat, a sombrero."

Now I'm telling him about my grandfather's "sense of hat," how I remember him sitting on a bench, studying his *Amsterdam News*, wearing his gray felt brim with the little red feather, down the street from the Harlem Y in Cruz's "old neighborhood New York," where writing painted on the wall by the playground still reads, "Harlem Plays the Best Ball in the World." Puerto Rican *pra-pras*, New York red beans and knishes—all survive in the urban Atlantis of Cruz's poetry, awaiting rediscovery.

(1991)

The Yellow House on the
Corner and Beyond

Rita Dove on the Edge of Domesticity

Of her first book, published in 1980 shortly after she had fin-
ished the Iowa Writer's Workshop, the poet Rita Dove said: "I
did conceive of [*The Yellow House on the Corner*] as a very domes-
tic title, but one on the edge of domesticity. I mean, the house
is on the corner. There's a sense of something beyond that—
outside of that boundary there is something else."[1] The persona
of the young Dove in her childhood home in Akron, Ohio,
thinking outward from within the house's parameters has mi-
grated through her work.[2] I am interested in Dove's first three
books and how her girlhood persona writes from within domes-
tic confines and then explodes their architecture, moving into
the outer space suggested by her own formidable mind. The
right to speak, in Dove's poems, is preceded by her articulation
of her right to think beyond the immediate world she lives in
and the limited expectations of a dominant culture.

Dove explores the public worlds of artifactual history as read-
ily as the private ones of family lore in her second book, *Mu-
seum*. But Dove defines an artifact as anything that is frozen by
memory.[3] This might as readily be Catherine of Siena, who in
the eponymous poem "walked the length of Italy / to find some-
one to talk to," or Dove's father's telescope. The poems of the
Pulitzer Prize–winning *Thomas and Beulah* reconstruct a family
history told in alternating narratives of characters modeled
after her grandparents. Dove has spoken of the challenge of sur-
rendering her voice to those of these characters; Beulah's do-
mestic narratives are faithful to a different order than those of
the poet's young persona. Still, the book, and Beulah's narra-

tive, explores that tension between confined domestic space and outside vistas. I will move first through Beulah's poems and then look at some of the girlhood poems in the rest of Dove's work.

Beulah's section of the book opens with her at work in the house in the poem called "Dusting." She is "patient among knickknacks," but as the stanza continues we see "the solarium a rage, / of light, a grainstorm / as her grey cloth brings / dark wood to life." Dusting, then, has transformative powers in a space where agitation and desire for change are atmospheric, despite Beulah's relative stillness. In "Sunday Greens" she dreams of change from inside her kitchen:

> She wants to hear
> wine pouring.
> She wants to taste
> change. She wants
> pride to roar through
> the kitchen till it shines
> like straw, she wants
>
> lean to replace
> tradition. Ham knocks
> in the pot, nothing
> but bones, each
> with its bracelet
> of flesh.
>
> The house stinks
> like a zoo in summer,
> while upstairs
> her man sleeps on.
> Robe slung over
> her arm and
> the cradled hymnal,
>
> she pauses, remembers
> her mother in a slip
> lost in blues,
> and those collards,
> wild-eared,
> singing.

By the end of the poem the wild-eared collard greens sing both Beulah's mother's blues and her own, domestic props in concert with a difficult search for voice. The kitchen muse has supplanted Beulah's own voice, the repeated "she wants" with which Dove ends lines and stanzas. The domestic landscape sings Beulah's blues on her behalf and in her stead. Crucially, Dove here has not used the powerful, first-person narrative of the poet's girlhood poems that I will examine shortly.

Beulah's half of the book ends with the poem "The Oriental Ballerina," in which a faded jewel-box dancer twirls in a tired and familiar bedroom. This ballerina "has not risen but drilled / a tunnel straight to America / where the bedrooms of the poor / are papered in vulgar flowers / on a background the color of grease, of / teabags, of cracked imitation walnut veneer." In Beulah's imagination the ballerina is exotic, from someplace else, from "the other side of the world." Dove's concentrated domestic imagery—here reminiscent of Gwendolyn Brooks— invokes the lived-in world at the same time as the imagined one. By the end of the poem at least one myth has been dissolved: "There is no China," Beulah thinks, but "above the stink of camphor, / the walls [are] exploding with shabby tutus." The female imagination exercised within the confines of a house has the power to rend the actual, physical structure to make space for something more transcendent, and is developed more thoroughly in the persona of the young girl growing up in Akron, Ohio, the Rita-Dove-as-poet-to-be in *The Yellow House on the Corner.*

The poems in that book are important for the way in which they mark different spaces in the house, and how the girl growing up inside imagines herself and the world she will come to inhabit. In "Geometry" she works a math problem:

> I prove a theorem and the house expands:
> the windows jerk free to hover near the ceiling,
> the ceiling floats away with a sigh.

The child is architect and carpenter, inhabiting physical and mental spaces so that she can build something else. The parts of the house metamorphose, "windows have hing[ed] into butterflies" until headed, like the windows, "to some point true and unproven." Once the house has been cleared away and made a blank slate of space, her mind can then be "out in the open," a free and unprecedented intellect in the making. In a recent interview Dove declared, "I hate to give people what they expect." We don't know what "people" she means, but certainly some readers might not expect to read about a young black girl engrossed in math problems and making the world that is her house disassemble in the process. She is dealing in the realm of utter mathematic truth in the first line; she proves the theorem, beyond all ambiguity, and once she has been able to make "true" an assemblage of numbers in space then she is conversely able to make her house disappear wall by wall, to make that physical environment "un-true," neither predefined nor ordained, thus watching and perhaps choosing to follow the newly winged windows, which fly "to some point true and unproven," perhaps the next intellectual plane for this young girl. The power of the iambic pentameter in the first line, "I prove a theorem and the house expands," is the sly joke of the poem; she leads with her high card as though to say, I can do this, watch me do this, both cleverly invoking and moving beyond an entire literary tradition that has rarely recognized the complex subjectivity of black girls. Dove will later work through the German language ("Epiphany is so much easier in German," she has said) because her father's books from World War II, in German, were the only three in the house she could not read while growing up. That sense, again, of a free-ranging intellect is part of the excitement that characterizes Dove's work.

Architecture is crucial in other frozen moments. In "A Suite for Augustus," when the young narrator descends the staircase to meet a suitor, the young man "stands penguin-still in a room / that's so quiet we forget it is there." The room is no longer her living room but a no-place in which the strange magic of her adolescence can occur. Just two stanzas later she is in an Ohio high school gymnasium but also altogether elsewhere, sighing, "Ah / Augustus, where did you learn to samba?" These no-places are the space of her imagination moving beyond its physical definitions. This might leave the young poet, in Brooks's words, "definitionless in this strict atmosphere," but it is that very state of definitionless-ness that is the starting point for a new and unimagined black female self.

Porches are inside and outside places at the same time, and they encode a whole realm of African-American mythological associations. In the architectural terms Dove so favors, the porch is both a space and not a space, and inside and outside at the same time so perhaps a no-person's space, or, space in transition. In "Grape Sherbert," "The diabetic grandmother / stares from the porch, a torch / of pure refusal." The porch is the space in which the grandmother can be both inside and outside of the family unit and of family members, who are enjoying homemade grape sherbert made from a guarded family recipe at a Memorial Day picnic, the sherbert that is "just how we imagined lavender / would taste." The rhyme of "porch" with torch, which for the subtle Dove is heavy-handed, suggests the force of the grandmother's anger and the instability of a porch that could go up in flames. Immediately after the grandmother's "pure refusal," the narrator contemplates ancestry:

> We thought no one was lying
> there under our feet,
> we thought it
> was a joke. I've been trying
> to remember the taste,
> but it doesn't exist.
> Now I see why
> you bothered,
> father.

Family history is both intangible and not, a taste that can't quite be recalled or a porch that might be burned down, as families encompass living disruptions as well as historical fissures and discontinuities.

"Adolescence II" articulates the least tangible aspects of budding sexuality:

> Although it is night, I sit in the bathroom, waiting.
> Sweat prickles behind my knees, the baby-breasts are alert.
> Venetian blinds slice up the moon, the tiles quiver in pale
>   strips.

Then they come, three seal men with eyes as round
As dinner plates and eyelashes like sharpened tines.
They bring the scent of licorice. One sits in the washbowl,

One on the bathtub edge; one leans against the door.
"Can you feel it yet?" they whisper.
I don't know what to say, again. They chuckle,

Patting their sleek bodies with their hands.
"Well, maybe next time." And they rise,
Glittering like pools of ink under moonlight.

And vanish, I clutch at the ragged holes
They leave behind, here at the edge of darkness.
Night rests like a ball of fur on my tongue.

What is striking in terms of this discussion is how the mystery of
impending adolescence as made the girl speechless in a space
markedly "definitionless" and therefore resistant to disassem-
bling. She does not know what to say; her mouth and body are
both full. The seal men do not enter and leave from windows or
even bathtub drains but mysteriously instead. Yet it is they who
mark the interior space—bathtub edge, washbowl, door—and
their metaphors are domestic, dinner plates and tines, ordinary
objects transformed just as the young girl is on the verge of one
of the few things the mind cannot control. So space is quite sud-
denly "pools of ink" and "ragged holes." The bathroom is no
longer the bathroom but the edge of darkness, in a melodra-
matic turn immediately undercut by the dazzlingly bizarre final
line, "Night rests like a ball of fur on my tongue." The atmos-
phere has shrunk to something small enough to fit in her
mouth, to take into her body as Dove metabolizes experience in
her work. The fur-ball "rests," is at home in her body, as this new
experience is part of her but also alien.

Dove quotes from Tracy Kidder's book *House* before the
poem in *Grace Notes*, "Genie's Prayer under the Kitchen Sink,"
which further illustrates her preoccupation with places in the
house. The poem is about an ornery, perennially out-of-favor
son whose relationship to his mother and the world is defined in
terms of his relationship to the workings of a house. The title of
the poem as a "Prayer" and Kidder's quote set the expectations:

"Housebuilding was conceived as a heroic effort to stop time, suspend decay and interrupt the ordained flow to ruin that started with Adam's fall." Genie, short for Eugene June Bug, has one withered leg and a nasty demeanor. His mother calls her "least-loved son" to fix a stopped-up kitchen sink and he comes, not because he loves her or because he should but because, as he says, "I came because I'm good at this, I'm good / with my hands." The second "I'm good" comes at the end of a line and a stanza and is both a part of its phrase, "I'm good with my hands" as well as a child's desperate attempt to convince himself, "I'm good at this, I'm good." Genie—and the play on that name should not be lost, as he works his wizardry under the sink— might be arm-deep in "hair and bacon grease" and "smashed radiant aluminum foil," but he is also dreaming elsewhere despite himself. The poem ends with his narrative, his Kilroy-was-here:

> I'm a man born too late for
> *Ain't that a shame,* I'm a monkey
> with a message and a heart like
> my father who fell laughing to his knees
> when it burst and 24 crows spilled
> from his mouth and they were all named Jim.
>
> When I'm finished here
> I'm gonna build a breezeway next,
> with real nice wicker and some astroturf.

Working with his hands on the house, the space beneath the sink becomes Genie's pulpit, the place where he laments and exalts and expands the space he is in. Dove charges the rhythm of that last line with vernacular energy, "with real nice wicker and some astroturf," which lets those ordinary materials, one natural and one quintessentially man-made, rise to the heroic heights suggested by the title and the epigraph. That same rhythmic, vernacular energy, which is one of Dove's flashy, seldom-brandished trump-cards, propels this final section and allows Genie to narrate his way out of his physical and structural constrictions.

The process of learning, and learning numbers, in particular, does not always make a space for freedom without cost, as it does in "Geometry." Dove's hard-earned and hard-imagined girlhood liberation is sometimes fraught with anxiety. Witness the whiz kid, the young Dove of "Flash Cards," from *Grace Notes:*

> In math I was the whiz kid, keeper
> of oranges and apples. *What you don't understand*
> *master,* my father said; the faster
> I answered, the faster they came.
>
> I could see one bud on the teacher's geranium,
> one clear bee sputtering at the wet pane.
> The tulip trees always dragged after heavy rain
> so I tucked my head as my boots slapped home.
>
> My father put up his feet after work
> and relaxed with a highball and *The Life of Lincoln.*
> After supper we drilled and I climbed the dark
>
> before sleep, before a thin voice hissed
> numbers as I spun on a wheel. I had to guess.
> Ten, I kept saying, *I'm only ten.*

The "answer," what makes the problem work and what proves the theorem, is a number, ten, which also gives us the answers as to why the child feels so much woe. The frozen, artifactual images: bee, geranium bud, tulip trees, are ossified in the moments between the answers, in caesuras between bites of quantifiable knowledge that sometimes yields answers, as with "ten," by accident. Dove has defined no spaces in this poem for purposes of disassembling; she is in fact trapped in no-space, spinning on a wheel with only the darkness instead of stairs to climb. While the father can lift his feet as she drags hers and can relax "with a highball and *The Life of Lincoln,*" there is no relaxation for the girl, for whom even sleep holds a "thin voice" that "hissed numbers." She suffers the true whiz kid's ultimate indignity: she has to guess rather than know, or prove. Forced to think and learn beyond her years, the space even of dreams in the home is no longer a free space and is beyond, in the moment of the poem, her control. More importantly, it seems that the girl is reacting strongly to a concept of learning as mastery and of dominion as the purpose of learning. She gives us the image of the father with his book, a man's entire life in his two hands, which underscores her attempt to resist this approach to intellectual activity, that one learns in order to possess.

"Fantasy and Science Fiction," from *Grace Notes,* opens with the dreamy girl looking out the front door of her parents' house to a house across the street. She is somewhere, if in her mind, moving through life within her family but also of her own volition. She says,

> Sometimes shutting a book and rising,
> you can walk off the back porch
> and into the sea—though
> it's not the sort of story
> You'd tell your mother.

This recalls the young girl grown who, while closer to Beulah's persona than to Dove's in "Summit Beach 1921," nonetheless remembers being a child who "climbed Papa's shed and stepped off / the tin roof into blue, / with her parasol and invisible wings." The difference between his young women and the persona of herself as a young girl that Dove has created is that young Dove needs neither wings nor parasol but rather the sheer power of her ravenous intellect to transport her between and beyond worlds.

In Dove's essay "The House that Jill Built" she recounts rereading her own books in a fit of writer's block anxiety.

> Why are so many women in my poems standing in rooms or at the threshold to rooms? Why are they so wistful? Why aren't they *doing* anything? Do I live only in the mind? And in the poem, "Upon reading Hölderlin on the Patio with the Aid of a Dictionary," why at the moment of her revelation, do I step out of my body?[4]

But it is precisely that power of the mind to transcend that is Dove's triumph. Her young women are always in some way leaving their homes, their physical spaces, either metaphorically or literally, and sometimes making their homes leave them. The lines and angles that make houses, the walls and doors and windows and measurements, are mastered in her own way by the black girl whiz kid learning math and imagining her own geometry of freedom. These poems are made by the Dove who understood that if she had various languages then she, too, could exist in multiple worlds simultaneously.

There is no iota of condescension from one who has moved ahead in these poems but rather a synthesis of confinement and transcendence, inside and outside, like porches. "Let's face it," Dove said,

> few of us were born in beautiful places. Yet I remember Akron, Ohio as a place of beauty. Rilke says in his *Letters to a Young Poet,* that if you cannot recount the riches of a place do not blame the place—blame yourself, because you are not rich enough to recall its riches. When I read that again, I realized that I'd be doing Akron an injustice if I would just dwell on its industrial ugliness, and if I could not explain or bring across some of its magic or make it come alive to others, then it was my problem, certainly not Akron's.[5]

Dove captures the paradox of so many growings-up in which we feed off our environments in both positive and negative ways, only to move and think beyond those childhood places. Dove manages to hold all of that at the same time, like a ball of fur on her poet's tongue, defined and amorphous, utterly implausible and utterly true, in the rooms of growing up and the planet of her imagination. "Just between / me and you, / woman to man," she says, as a grown woman to her father in the poem "Anti-Father," "outer space is / inconceivably / intimate."

(1991)

The One Who Went Before and
Showed the Way
Remembering August Wilson

Something was happening in New Haven, Connecticut, in the spring of 1984. Creative black people seemed to be everywhere, in earnest conversation over endless cups of coffee, talking big and doing big, believing in culture and its power and possibility. The Afro-American Cultural Center at Yale—then and now known affectionately as the House—opened its doors to this burgeoning creativity. As a college senior at the time, I was editing a magazine based at the House called *Ritual and Dissent,* and today I am amazed when I look in its pages: original interviews, conducted that year in New Haven, with Wole Soyinka, Audre Lorde, and Melvin Dixon as well as stories and poems and reviews by writers and scholars who went on to do great work, all of us products of that remarkable time and place.

That spring came a play by a new playwright named August Wilson. We'd see him around New Haven, wearing some variety of old-school hat, drinking coffee, and writing in notebooks, or sitting quietly in the back of rehearsals, many of which were held right at the House. Angela Bassett and Charles "Roc" Dutton had performed scenes from Shakespeare at the House; its imposing, Gothic "enormous room" was beautifully suited to theater. Now in that same space, as well as at the University School of Drama, with those same actors and others, Lloyd Richards was rehearsing the Wilson play.

Of course we all knew who Lloyd Richards was. The legendary director was not only dean of the Yale School of Drama at the time but also the director of the 1959 Broadway production of Lorraine Hansberry's *A Raisin in the Sun,* starring Sidney

Poitier, Diana Sands, Ruby Dee, and others in the black theater firmament. He was American theater royalty and a black theater deity. But this playwright, this new guy, this August Wilson, was something else, working right here in our hothouse. Even as a college senior, I knew when the curtain fell on those first performances of *Ma Rainey's Black Bottom* that something not just important but shifting had happened. We'd spent two hours (or probably three or four, because Wilson plays run famously long in their early incarnations) in a Chicago recording studio in the 1920s, at the dawn of recorded jazz and blues and thus a new era for African-American popular culture, and we had listened to characters with historical integrity talk, really talk, about profound issues of black progress. No matter the decade, no matter the characters, all of August Wilson's plays ask black people: Where do we go from here? What is progress? Can we do it together? What is our inheritance? Lest you imagine that talk as dissertational, however, August Wilson makes characters named Slow Drag and Levee and Toledo and Cutler woof, lie, and signify, in the great oral tradition of Negro talk in the spaces we've made our own.

I went to the premiere of *Radio Golf* at the Yale Repertory Theater in the spring of 2005. It would be Wilson's last opening in New Haven before his death at age sixty on October 2 of that year, and the play was the tenth and final of his twentieth-century cycle. The curtain came up on the same stage where I'd seen *Ma Rainey*. This time the milieu (for in Wilson's plays, workplaces were spaces where human beings speak their minds and hearts) was an office in which people came in and out singing their arias (metaphorically speaking), and the same questions were raised, approached from different angles: What does black progress mean if it does not attempt to bring along a community and respect a community? What do we need to know and bring forward from our history? And why is none of this a straightforward enterprise? In *Radio Golf*, the discursive tug of war (or the rational distance) between Harmon Wilks and Elder Joseph Barlow does not yield easy or immediate answers to these questions. This is apt, for we have not yet overcome, nor have we reached the promised land. The play ends on a hopeful note, with family ties revealed between the "progress-seeking" bourgeoisie and the materially dispossessed "folk." Wilson sees black people of different classes as necessarily connected. The folk character in this play gets all the good lines, but he does not have the answers. Difficult interactions across class lines move the community closer together—connections made tenuously, perhaps, with the string and Scotch tape of conversation.

In Elder Joseph Barlow we have a familiar Wilson type: the street poet, corner philosopher, mother wit, or half-wit character he writes like no one else. Wilson understood the street-corner poets with rural southern roots who abound in urban America, and he imbues them with a southern sense of the aphoristic and the mysterious, that kind of hyperbole and non sequitur that tends toward wisdom. "I want my ham!" is a cri de coeur from his play *Two Trains Running*, and it is not just idle exclamation, but an existential howl, time signature, grace note, cypher. Levee's obsession with his footwear in *Ma Rainey's Black Bottom* shows us that a pair of shoes is not always only a pair of shoes. Wilson understood the symbolic dimensions in which everyday life presents itself to us if we pay attention. The metaphorical is ever present, which is to say that life and its lessons are not always best apprehended straight on but rather after the groundwork of associative thinking or attuned listening. When, in the play *Fences*, Troy Maxson makes his speech about fences, we understand how the most quotidian and familiar objects give us a way to think about historical wrongs and the complex pride of character. In all Wilson's plays, the men, especially, strive for dignity, despite the soul-crushing challenges they face and have faced for generations.

In *The Piano Lesson*, Wilson asks what we, as black people, do with our cultural and familial legacies, symbolized in the play by an elaborately carved piano whose decoration tells a story reaching back to slavery. He asks the question about black people in a specific historical context, and that is part of what is extraordinary about his work. While white people—indeed anybody—can, of course, hear the question and appreciate the plays, he is speaking to black people, without winks or smiles, dilution or translation. What to do with our cultural legacy is, ultimately, our question. How families remember is our question. The press of history and its challenges is always present in a Wilson play, but he uses history to situate us in a moment where we might ask what we are to do next. *So high, you can't get over it / so low you can't get under it / so wide, you can't go around it. You gotta come in at the door.* That is the truth of history.

When writing is called poetic, it usually means something conventionally beautiful and mellifluous in style. I would call Wilson a poetic writer in the way he understands the poetics of speech and how he recognizes the potent allusiveness of conversation. The stage directions that open *Ma Rainey's Black Bottom* point to the kind of rich talk to come and also to the grand historical sweep in which Wilson worked: "Chicago in 1927 is a rough city, a bruising city, a city of millionaires and derelicts, gangsters and roughhouse dandies, whores and Irish grandmothers who move through its streets fingering long black rosaries. Somewhere a man is wrestling with the taste of a woman in his cheek. Somewhere a dog is barking. Somewhere the moon has fallen through the window and broken into thirty pieces of silver." Spoken language is rich and nuanced and oratorical in the traditions of black talk Wilson feeds on, and thus is his prose poetic.

One aspect of African-American history is a melancholia that comes from the interruption—the violent fissure of the Middle Passage and its subsequent soul-annihilating indignities. The never-to-be-resolved fissure, the never-to-be-known homeland, coexist with the great possibilities of reinvention that gave the world jazz and blues, music heavily influenced by African music but utterly, yes, purely, completely, African-American, which is to say American. Our death came at the bottom of the ocean and then at the hands of the brutal slave system and then from the privations of Jim Crow, and then at the hands of the police and of each other. That's a lot of unending blues. Wilson is always attuned to the "sea of bones": that it is there, that it is unresolved, that it is a crossroads, that it presses on the present, that it forms a hieroglyphics that the griot needs to unlock in order to prophesy.

I think of poet Gwendolyn Brooks's wonderful words—"I am a black. I am one of the Blacks. We occur everywhere. Don't call me out of my name"—and her wish that to be called black links her to other African people, diasporized and not. Does that linkage hold? Is our wish for it to hold sentimental? What is the motherland that each of us may wish for, and what does it mean to try to heal that need with words, deeds, and culture, our bottle trees and shell-studded graves? Wilson's genius as a writer was his ability to keep the listening ear open, both for the literal sounds of the oral tradition he clearly loved as well as for a proverbial logic and structure that must be called African. In grappling with the literary possibilities of a realist theater, trying consistently to bring the spoken word into the written form, Wilson consistently brought the genius of African-American language into his plays.

In some ways, August Wilson doesn't feel like a writer of the 1980s, a decade not known for its attention to history in art. But it was in the eighties—when so much was new, when theory and multiculturalism were changing the arts dramatically, when the shape of art went in a million different directions—that Wilson began his untrendy but radical project of looking to the past. It took vision to recognize, as he did, that until we examine our history we will not be able to look or move forward. And looking at that history is also how we come to recognize our seers. In a ravishing speech about "the secret of life" in *Joe Turner's Come and Gone,* the root-worker Bynum Walker says: "[M]y daddy taught me the meaning of this thing that I had seen and showed me how to find my song. He told me he was the One Who Goes Before and Shows the Way. Said there was lots of shiny men and if I ever saw one again before I died then I would know that my song had been accepted and worked its full power in the world and I could lay down and die a happy man. A man who done left his mark on life . . . So I takes the power of my song and binds [people] together." Some part of the artist knew that the moment had come when the century could be surveyed, intimately and in the terms and language of black urban folks whose wisdom was sometimes practical and sometimes potently mystical.

Wilson audaciously redefined the American theater canon in just twenty-five years. He finished the cycle he began, one play for each decade of the twentieth century, and while it does not make up for his absence from our midst, let alone for the absent promise of more words, he chiseled something in granite that will stand like Shakespeare. I wonder what he might have said about evanescence and black culture, the way so much of our genius is neglected or misnamed, misplaced, destroyed. Wilson's genius is at hand; he built his own boat to last.

I am satisfied to have watched him from a short distance twenty-five years ago and to be able to say today that I was right: something very important was happening. This was a shiny man, humbly telling the village's tales. He revered the word, and the brilliance with which black people have shaped it. He knew a good story when he saw one. His narrative sense was unerring. He loved black people enough to celebrate us and challenge us. Loving black people to my mind means loving humanity. My favorite-ever quote of his—and he made many rich and profound statements—is one that makes me catch my breath before writing, humble before the task at hand and also wild-eyed with the excitement and ambition his words inspire. He said, "You have responsibilities as a global citizen. Your history dictates your duty. And by writing about black people, you are not limiting yourself. The experiences of African-Americans are as wide open as God's closet."

In his work and in his deeds, August Wilson was what the old folks call a righteous man.

(2006)

Bill T. Jones *Still/Here*

Gwendolyn Brooks's poem "Infirm" is a prayer that precisely names Bill T. Jones's overall project:

> Everybody here
> is infirm.
> Everybody here is infirm.
> Oh. Mend me. Mend me. Lord.

Though the AIDS crisis provides impetus and subject matter for much of Jones's work, he forms essential and enduring questions that have wide-reaching relevance. As Brooks reminds us "we are all infirm," in Jones's work mortality twinned with fierce living is the common denominator of the polis. Regarding his dance *Still/Here,* Jones wrote, "[T]he resources necessary to cope with life-threatening illnesses are the same as those necessary for truly owning one's life." The work explores the ways that we are simultaneously mortal and fully alive.

I don't think I fully understood that dichotomy in the 1980s, when the epidemic was the urgency everywhere and it seemed we were always waiting for the other shoe to drop. "HIV-positive" means something different now than it did in the eighties or in 1993, when Jones made *Still/Here.* Remembering the mideighties for me is remembering being part of a dancing community in Washington, D.C. So many of those men are now dead of AIDS-related illnesses, lustrous young black men like Eddie and David, big brothers, tutors in fabulosity who spun, glittered, and never grew old. Jones's still/here dancing body testifies to something else: endurance, work, self-care, scientific progress, perhaps genetics, sheer good fortune, so much I do not know. His creative process works toward the truest questions and then builds a movement vocabulary from the kinetic explorations of those questions. Rather than ask, Do you believe in God? he asks, What does your god look like? Now there is a question. He understands physical gesture profoundly, turning quotidian gestures into things danced, repeatable, and iconic.

Jones continually returns to community, its struggle and best hope. *Still/Here* shows so many moments where communities form and fray. A woman who has just received an HIV-positive diagnosis surrenders to the arms of friends, then wrenches away. A man whose mother has just died of cancer argues bitterly with an aunt, flat hands turned palm-side out to deflect her words, protecting the vulnerable throat. Knots of bodies fall together then fling apart. But Jones continues to arrange dancers in circles and move bodies in relationship to one another. The movements of his soloists are beautiful and rich, but most interesting, and persistent, is when and how he brings those individuals imperfectly, infirmly, together.

Jones is a gorgeous dancer, but he is not a supersonic dancer. The whisper of stiffness in his body's movement articulates the aspect of dance and living that is strive, sweat, aspiration, and hope. Danced beauty need not be solely supersonic. I imagine what it feels like to be in his body, warming it in the morning, bringing it to suppleness and up to the expressive challenges of the day. I feel similar emotion in watching Baryshnikov dance now, the famously supersonic body now compromised by injury but finding in contemporary modern dance a movement vocabulary that in part allows us to witness the creep of mortality that does not eclipse the need to dance. As my own body remembers all that it can no longer execute, I remember my dancing friends, that community, ever-reconvened in Jones's work, his circles of human beings. Who among us is not in some way infirm, patched back together, and still/here?

(2005)

II

Black Feminist Thinking

My Grandmother's Hair

Imagine a black woman in 1925 who wanted to be a scholar. The first black woman received her Ph.D. in 1923; the first crop of black women Ph.D.s—Otelia Cromwell, Eva P. Dykes, Georgina Shepherd, and Anna Julia Cooper (who earned the degree at the age of sixty-seven)—went on to work as teachers in black high schools because discrimination prevented them from teaching at universities. So the black woman who wanted to be a scholar was simultaneously inventing herself and blazing a brand-new trail. Now imagine that woman wanted to study the black body—that which has so persistently been reduced to perverse stereotype—and who believed its study could teach black people something important about themselves. What would it mean to scrutinize the disarticulated black body with love, to put it back together, in a sense, and do a new arithmetic that attempts to bring light to the study of who we are? What would it mean to disentangle this enterprise from concurrent work that saw "black" bodies as grotesquely racialized and emblematic? What of a black woman in the 1920s who became an anthropologist, one of the first of her race or gender in a field where she was more likely to be among the studied than the studiers? And what of that black woman anthropologist turning the calipers on her own people? What did she think she would discover?[1]

The history of the violent isolation of body parts is too extensive to accede to the notion that parts can tell us anything about the whole and that the individual whole can tell us anything about the body politic, its putative essence. Think of the macabre American practice of selling souvenir black body parts in the market after lynchings. How much for a finger, an ear, a penis? A basket of fingers, a garland of ears, the severed penis a symbol of feared black masculine power in its most mythical bloom. Chopped-off black hands in the Congo, bits of dissected Khoi genitalia in the Musée de l'Homme in Paris, parts displayed as object lessons, pieces standing for the whole, often in the name of "science." Yet we want to know ourselves better and long for science and epistemology that will help us think about Us.

Such was the mission of a black woman anthropologist called Caroline Bond Day. In 1932 when she graduated from Harvard, she became the first woman of any color to earn a master's degree in physical anthropology. At the time, to the best of my knowledge, there were only two other African-American women who had studied or were studying anthropology: Zora Neale Hurston, who studied at Barnard College with Franz Boas and whose work was published in 1933 in *Mules and Men,* and Katherine Dunham, who was studying at Northwestern University in Chicago with Melville Herskovits and who published her research on Haiti and Jamaica in *Journey to Accompong* and *Island Possessed.* Day's thesis, *A Study of Some Negro White Families in the United States,* was published in 1932 by the Harvard African Series. These three women had no predecessors in their field.[2]

When I was a child I loved looking at the books on my parent's shelves, and *A Study of Some Negro White Families* was one that I returned to time and again. The book chronicled over three hundred families of mixed black and white ancestry using the methodologies of physical anthropology available at the time— the measurement of skull widths, nose breadths, hair texture, and so forth—along with sociological inquiry into subjects home, work, and social habits. Who were these people sitting on porches with their high white collars and crocheted shawls, their voluminous hair arranged carefully, people named Archibald and Florida, Nancy and Josephine, Ulysses, Nellie, Sinai, Etnah, Daisy, Augustus, and Inez? Within *A Study's* pages what most compelled me were the photographs, many taken by Day herself, not only of her subjects but of their hair. Under each portrait and hair sample was a racial breakdown, fractions of "N" (Negro), "W" (White), and "I" (Indian) in the subject's racial makeup. This information was ascertained through interviews and knowledge of family history, but the racial combinations marked the pictures of the hair samples so that they became representative of racial types. Hair was described along a spectrum from "frizzled" to "curly" to "deep waves" to "low waves" to "perfectly straight." Day wrote of the extreme mutability of hair textures and emphasized, "It is doubtful if two people are ever seen with hair which is exactly alike" (12).

The book amazed me. It was strange. It was discomfiting. It was unlike anything I had ever seen, nor have seen since. It seemed to both expose the secret lives of black people and yet conceal further secrets behind its pages. In some profound way it seemed both right and wrong at the same time. There were notable names amongst the family trees: W. E. B. DuBois ($\frac{5}{8}$ N, $\frac{3}{8}$ W, according to Day), Josephine St. Pierre Ruffin ($\frac{3}{8}$ N, $\frac{1}{8}$ I, $\frac{4}{8}$ W), artist Laura Wheeler Waring ($\frac{4}{8}$ N, $\frac{1}{8}$ I, $\frac{3}{8}$ W), civic leader Walter White ($\frac{5}{32}$ N, $\frac{1}{32}$ I, $\frac{26}{32}$ W), opera singer Lillian Evans (nee Evanti) ($\frac{7}{16}$ N, $\frac{9}{16}$ W). Its pages led me to think about myself as an adolescent, about what my own bloodlines "added up to." I liked the structure of proper family trees, the lines and branches that connect. I would ruminate on the stopping point, the ancestor beyond which we could not go where the information stopped. Often, of course, it stopped where the slave ships let off, on the shores of the United States. Day's charts stopped with supposedly "pure" racial types, the full blood African, or Indian or Caucasian, who was always a man. I cut a snippet of my own hair and tried to hold it together next to the samples. What might I be? Did my hair reflect my "blood"?

We owned this esoteric book because Day was my grandmother's older half-sister, my mother's Aunt Carrie, my own Great Aunt. She had died when my mother was a girl, but growing up I heard many stories about her. My grandmother revered "Sister" and found in her a model for a life of intellectual engagement and of service to others—both sisters were social workers for many years. Aunt Carrie also offered a model of independence within the conventions of black middle-class society. Her working papers are kept in the Peabody Museum of Harvard University, donated in 1931 by Day's professor, Earnest A. Hooten. They are the only extant working notes of a project undertaken by a black woman at that time. The archive contains the cards on which Day kept notes and measurements on the physiognomy of her 2,537 subjects. There are large, careful charts and family trees. Perhaps most fascinating is her correspondence with her subjects. In these letters was see her energy and tenacity—she pursued the project over a decade, through serious illness, other jobs, and geographical dispersal. We see the extent of her social network—her subjects were often people she knew, so letters not only address the business at hand but also the affairs of the day. She consults "older people in the community who were not related but whose unofficial business it was, seemingly, to remember the ancestry of everybody else" (5). And her own powers of persuasion are evident, not least of all when the thorny issue of racial "passing." Bond's work seems to have been supported in its initial stages, and her subjects often noted their pride in supporting the work of one of "their" women endorsed by a grant at Harvard University. But when Day wrote people again to ask permission to publish her findings, objections frequently arose. "My brother is strictly w——in Boston," one wrote, "you understand."[3] Other subjects were described as fearful of exposure because they were "passing for white" or had "gone to the other side." Day notes, "Of 346 families, 35 of the families state that there are one or more members who "are 'passing,' either entirely, or only temporarily for purposes of obtaining lucrative employment" (5). She then says she knows of 50 more families with members passing who were not part of her study and writes, "[P]ractically every family with whom I have talked can give me an additional few names" (11).

Day developed her own methodological quirks that illustrate the ways in which this was inquiry that could only have been conducted from within the group being studied. With regard to the hair samples, for example, Day notes that "errors due to artificial straightening were partly eliminated by Mrs. Day, who knew most of the subjects and had notes on their true hair form" (13). The work gives a sense of the lived reality of the acute gaze with which people try to read physical racial signs, and the extent to which those markers delimited human experience and definition.

Day is careful to talk about her attempts to make a cross-section, class-wise, of black communities. She was explicit that she did not want the achievements of many members of her group "to argue for the advantages of race-crossing, it is my firm belief that Negroes who are of unmixed blood are just as capable of achievement along all lines as those who are mixed" (6). She seemed to understand the bias and misuse of the work she was doing, and the danger of any "reading of the body."

Day's anthropology would not hold up against what we now know about race and biology. She often mixed what we would call sociology with hard science, imagining certain traits as representative. What did the metaphorical tea leaves of physiognomy suggest to her? In the end, for me, the Caroline Bond Day project is about a young black woman trying to move beyond received ideas about race, to do more than follow hunches but rather let a relatively new science tell her things she did not already know. Day nudged her social group, many of whom did not want to be pushed or investigated, to tell their stories and reveal secrets that might be helpful to a broader understanding. That she made black people believe that having their bodies calibrated and measured, their very body hair snipped and analyzed and saved, would tell them something they did not know, seems simultaneously discomforting, audacious, and visionary to me, especially when we look at the state of the "art" and "science" involved with the boom in DNA ancestry research today. It is as though Day imagined the disarticulated black body could be put back together again, in a new light moving towards new conclusions about what she herself already knew: the full span of Negro endowment and achievement.

Day's work also offers a glimpse "within the veil," as DuBois would have put it, to a world that exists in lore and that has been passed on, refigured as something else, and often, vanished completely, as those old-fashioned names have, too. Sometimes we may still "read" racially ambiguous bodies, looking for that telltale frizzle at the hairline, shadow curling around the rim of an ear, a breadth of facial feature that tells what the body's occupant wishes silenced. It's still a mystery, this thinking about "the Logan head," "my mother's hips," "my father's nose," when the body parts in question are thought to be racialized ones.

Now we can send a tissue scraping from inside our cheeks or a strand of hair to various sites that analyze our DNA and tell something of what Day was aiming for: what percentage this, that, and the other we are, right down to where in Africa our people might have come from. The wish to go beyond where the family tree stops can be powerful in any of us. Imagination takes us, and sometimes desire takes us as well. The urge to know is I daresay natural, but what we make of it is tellingly romantic, a way of explaining ourselves. "Send your hair to Howard," says a friend, in a compressed shorthand that also glories in the fact that a historically black school is a place where through an object as ephemeral as a strand of hair one could come closer to knowing what has been systematically suppressed and eradicated over hundreds of years. In describing a characteristic of her family tree, my mother sometimes says, there were the narrow-headed Logans and the round-headed Logans. She didn't elaborate on what that meant, but it was a way of understanding ourselves visually as part of a lineage, part of a primordial survival fantasy wherein you would "know your people" anywhere you saw them, know where you belonged.

It comes down for me to Aunt Carrie, to telling her story without trying to draw lessons from it or to crisply lay out what is applicable in the present. Caroline Bond Day believed that the knowledge that was out there could help her let the world at large know about a proud community that was invisible. She believed that with this physical data she could disprove myths of Negro inferiority by first showing Negroes existed in diversity and then writing about who lived in those bodies, their quotidian habits and accomplishments. And I think as a social scientist who quested to get her work done for over ten years, she also believed in the scholar's first tenet: pursue what you do not know. That she herself was by type and in fact one of the subjects only makes the quest to know more, from the inside, ever more poignant and exemplary.

There was one thing left to check on my trip to the Peabody archive: the hair samples. Amazingly, they are there, folded four times into pieces of white paper, the hair, hundreds of cuttings from people in her study, cuttings she photographed and then put on pages indicating the racial mixture: ¼ N, ¼ I, ½ white, hair of differing degrees of length, bend, curl, and frizzle, shine, smudges of hair like smoke, hanks of shiny hair marked "¾ I," boxes full of nearly hundred-year-old hair.

Properly, the hair shouldn't be kept at the Peabody, the archivist told me. Organic material must be kept elsewhere. So needless to say, I wasn't to touch the hair, or look at the lot of it.

But I had to see the hair of one of Caroline Bond Day's subjects in particular: her half-sister, Wenonah Bond, nineteen years old in 1927 when the sample was clipped, my grandmother.

What can I say about sitting in an archive at Harvard University holding a piece of my grandmother's hair? In the thirty-one years we shared I was her treasure. She brushed and braided my own hair throughout my childhood—she would have said she "disciplined" my hair—working the ends of my pigtails around a spit-moistened index finger and oiling the frizzling edges. In adulthood, she kept her own hair carefully set and arranged. It was blue-gray and lustrous all the years I knew her. When she died at eighty-six, the last thing I did in her presence, in the presence of her body, was stroke her beautiful hair, which felt wavy and soft as it always had and slightly crisped with hairspray. She had been dead for an hour. Her spirit was still in the room but was quickly leaving, and we could feel it, and that was that. It was time to go.

Her hair, now before me. It was the same color as mine at nineteen: dark brown with a slight reddish undertone, not as curly as mine, a bit mussy, as befits a young woman on the go, as she was then, away from Washington, D.C., from inevitable Teacher's College and early, imminent marriage, from the further South of most of the people she knew and came from, toward learning and Sister and all the possibilities she enacted and represented.

I touched the hair, though I was not supposed to. I am reverent about libraries and archives and their rules, so I justified my transgression with the thought that I was the only person on earth who might ever need to touch this particular hank of hair. Oh, my Nana, there you are. Here is your hair between my fingers. My mind went to an odd place, to a book I'd recently read with my children, about extinct ice age wooly mammoths. One was discovered in Siberia, frozen for tens of thousands of years in a block of ice. Paleontologists used hair dryers to meticulously defrost small parts of it, so they could snip a bit of fur and see if they could find an unbroken strand of fragile woolly mammoth DNA. As the dryers melted the ice, the book said, the refrigerated research room filled with the musky animal smell of the thousands-year-old creature. If they found that unbroken strand, for which they still search, would they try to clone another wooly mammoth and place it in the paleontological park now under development? Why would you, if you could, and why wouldn't you?

I held my grandmother's hair, which felt like the end of her, except, stranger still, it was the before of her, before I knew her, before she even had a child who would be my mother. This was a Wenonah Bond I never knew, nor did my mother. No, not Wenonah. A hank of her hair at nineteen, according to her sister's notations, ½ Negro, ¼ Indian, ¼ White. What does it, what could it possibly, tell me?

Taking care not to disturb its pattern, I put the cutting back into the paper and folded the packet four times and returned it back to the archivist, who put it in a glassine envelope in an acid-free box in a basement at the Peabody Museum at Harvard University, where it remains, in the Caroline Bond Day Papers.

"Imitations of Life"?

*A Very Short History of Black Women and Food
in Popular Iconography from Jemima to Oprah,
or, When Is a Pancake Not Just a Pancake?*

> [W]hen Oprah got thin . . . her personality went down
> the drain with it. She used to remind me of Aunt
> Jemima—I kind of liked her. Then when she was
> trying to look like Janet Jackson it didn't work.

The source may be suspect—Jackie Stallone, cuckoo-bird
mother to Sylvester—but the comment above nonetheless crys-
tallizes the stubborn prevalence of certain images of black
women with which white America has long been comfortable.
Much has been said about the Jemima (Oprah)—Jezebel (Janet,
when she gets thin) iconographic dichotomy: either black
women are overweight, desexualized "mammy" figures who exist
to provide succor for white families (at the expense of their
own), or they are hypersexualized Jezebels, dusky temptresses
who threaten the white family and justify white male rapacious-
ness and desire. This dichotomy is not only historical; as the Stal-
lone quote illustrates—and, by the way, this was stated in pre-
cisely the same terms by David Letterman and Paul Schaefer on
Letterman's late night television program as well as doubtlessly
in other sources I have not come across—the mammy stereotype
is at work, if altered to suit the times, in America today. To cite
just one example, Patricia Hill Collins uses Rhetaugh Dumas's
study of black women in corporate America to describe how
those women are penalized "if they don't appear warm and
nurturing."[1] Collins continues, "[T]he mammy symbolizes the
dominant group's perception of the ideal Black female relation-
ship to elite white male power." The first black woman to win an

Academy Award was Hattie McDaniels, for her 1939 portrayal of a character named Mammy who kept her white mistress going in *Gone with the Wind*. Some fifty years later, Whoopi Goldberg was rewarded for her portrayal of the psychic Oda Mae who, while not a "classic" mammy figure nonetheless devotes her time— what do we learn about her life separate from the quest to re-unite the dead Sam with Molly? What do we know of her hopes and desires?—to the bringing together and tending of the white heterosexual family. When Halle Berry became the first black woman to win a best actress award, in 2002, discussion rarely strayed from speculation that she won because she took her clothes off in a graphic sex scene with a white man. We might call this victory the revenge of Jezebel.

But what we are considering here is not the mammy or Jezebel figures per se—there is some excellent scholarship on the matter that carefully charts distinctions between the mammy, the Jemima, the black matriarch, et cetera—but the ways in which food is coded on black women's bodies. The 1934 film version of Fannie Hurst's novel *Imitation of Life* could be seen as the invention of Aunt Jemima were it not for the fact that Jemima was at that point long-alive and well in the American imagination, since the Chicago World's Fair in 1893. The film was so swollen with discomfiting stereotypes it offered a rash of possible titles for this essay, including "Your supper's ready, Miss Bea," to "I'se your cook and I wanna stay your cook," to "You're gonna make your pancakes and I'm gonna sell them." A glance at the film lets us consider black women's bodies, food, and the popular imagination.

The story as directed by John Stahl can be briefly summarized: Bea is a recently widowed white woman with a small daughter, Jessie, to support. She has taken over her husband's maple syrup business. The film opens in sanitized domestic chaos: the child is in the bathtub whining, "I want my quack-quack" while her mother answers phones, agrees to make impossible deliveries of maple syrup, and burns breakfast. A black woman, Delilah, appears at her back door, at the wrong address to answer an ad for a "girl." All she wants, she says, is a place for herself and her little girl—Peola, tragic mulatta extraordinaire, we'll discover—to live; she'll work for practically nothing, she says. Bea is about to send her on her way when screams and splashes erupt upstairs; Jessie has fallen into the tub. When Bea brings a retrieved, dried, and dressed Jessie downstairs, Delilah has established her place in the kitchen and the culture of food: the table is set, milk is poured, and breakfast is on its way. Delilah pleads again to stay, saying: "Oh, don't worry about food. Peola's so little, she don't hardly eat nothin'. And I'se very deceiving as to proportions. I'm very light at the table . . . I don't eat like I look, it's the truth." Bea—played by a slim Claudette Colbert—replies, "You're just two hundred pounds of mother fighting to keep her baby," and then Delilah says, with the huge smile that will be used to sell 32 million pancakes, "two-hundred and forty." Delilah instantly becomes the "family" feeder, both emotionally and as raw labor on which Bea survives.

Bea raves about the pancakes Delilah prepares and asks, What's the secret. Delilah replies that it's her grandmother's secret, passed down to Delilah's mother, who was "famous for her pancakes." Delilah swears it's the one secret she'll take to the grave, but in a matter of seconds she is whispering it in Bea's ear. Bea responds, "That's all?" and bolts up from the table and out the door to begin the process of opening a Boardwalk store in which "Aunt Delilah's Pancakes" will be sold. The culinary secret is both precious to Delilah and part of her black and female legacy; not only is the implausible idiocy of giving away her idea presented as guileless generosity, the black female legacy itself is trivialized in the film, reduced to a secret so simplistic it can be given away in a moment.

Delilah's image is used to call up "authenticity" and the comfort both of warm, sweet carbohydrates as well as of the invoked "good old days" of slavery and a maintained social order in which the place of black women is tending the white family. In an 1896 advertisement for Aunt Jemima pancakes, her face is reproduced over and over again to sell the product. This and so many other stereotypical images of black women have made millions of dollars of which she has no part. In this advertisement the imagined history of Aunt Jemima—"send four cents in stamps for life history of Aunt Jemima; and her pickaninny dolls," read the ad—is part and parcel of the selling and marketing of the product. The body on display is yoked to the food it prepares, but that invented history bears no actual resemblance to the lives of black women and the food they prepare. Her smiling image is reproduced over and over and over again to guarantee, as the ad reads, "a sterling product . . . genuine." This iconography is replicated in *Imitation of Life*. By the end of the film Delilah's image has gone from a single painted sign, to thousands of boxes of pancake mix, to a huge, neon deity in which an animated "Aunt Delilah" flips pancakes: "32 million sold."

To continue, an out-of-work, alcoholic white male character appears to offer Bea two magic words about the pancake mix: "Box it," and when he and Bea tell Delilah the company is going to incorporate and offer her 20 percent of her own property—of her own property!—Delilah wails that she wants neither money, car, nor home of her own, she wants only to stay with and take care of "Miss Bea." Her sole request for recompense is for the lavish funeral of her dreams. As she gives away, then, her claim to her own business, the white man replies, "Once a pancake, always a pancake." This represents a complete elision of the woman with the food product; Delilah is like the pancake itself, round and brown and utterly implacable, never speaking back, constant, but nonetheless the absolute spine of the film's economy.

What to make, then, of the fact that this mammy feeds everyone but never herself, is "deceiving as to proportions"? Her large body tells one story and hides another. The imagined history of that body—how is it that white Bea is literally half the size of black Delilah if she's always eating pancakes?—belies the actual history of a woman who, like any other, has an imaginary life, a private life out of the sight of white people, who sleeps, dreams, and eats. That actual history is occluded, just as the bodily history of black women as rape victims is so often erased so that the image of the lunched black male body can take its place when we talk about the history of physical violation of black people in the name of race.

The black female body that is overweight but does not eat is a body stripped of immediate, actual history at the same time that it is mired in the imagined history of stereotypes. Either Delilah is eating off-screen—how else would she survive, let alone occupy the physical space she does?—or she is not a human being. Both possibilities jibe with the dehumanizing effects of these images. Oprah Winfrey's first famous, public weight loss came as a result of a nonfood, liquid diet, so she was never associated with foods figured as "diet foods": salad, broiled sole, and the like. We can read those as twentieth-century white lady foods, inscribed by gender, race, and class. Around the time of *Imitation of Life*, *Photoplay* magazine reported that Joan Crawford's favorite diet food was saltines spread with mustard. Since Winfrey lost her weight that first time in public without eating at all she remains tied to the comfort foods we are meant to think made her heavy in the first place—the mashed potatoes bearing her name on the menu of The Eccentric, the Chicago restaurant in which she once invested, as well as the various delicacies she has told us she loves. Those foods can then remain pathologized, in a sense, as fat black woman foods. In *USA Today* around the time of Winfrey's first big reduction, white triathlete Jeff Greenman invoked Oprah Winfrey to talk about his own weight loss. He dieted eating "vegetables, lean meat, and fish. It was no Oprah diet." Of course, we don't see white men invoking Oprah's name in *USA Today* to discuss the success of their film studios, or of their climb into multimillion dollar, self-made status.

This is part of what is so fascinating about the "mammy-izing" of Oprah on her talk show, an ample black bosom on which white America weeps: her access to the shaping of images of black women is unprecedented; she is not visible solely in stereotypical terms. She is the only black woman ever to own a TV and movie production studio—Harpo, where her television talk show is produced—and after Lucille Ball and Mary Pickford, is only the third woman ever. The December 1991 issue of *Working Woman* magazine, in an article that charts both the physical and financial evolution of Winfrey and what would seem to be her iconographic opposite, Madonna, estimates that Winfrey by the end of 1991 brought in 39 million dollars in revenue from her TV talk show—seen on some two hundred television stations in the United States and in thirty-four foreign countries—and Harpo studio. She is the first black female billionaire, and only the third self-made female billionaire in history. Most crucially, she produced 220 hours of new television programming in 1991, which represents a great deal of space in which to construct and mold the images of black women. One mass media study observes, "The amount of viewing just commercials [by a twelve-year-old child in a given year] would be sufficient for even adults to learn a language or learn how to fly an airplane. . . . When one realizes that by twelfth grade a child has spent more time before a TV set than he has in school, one can appreciate the possible influence in molding behavior."[2] Winfrey has purchased the rights to Zora Neale Hurston's *Their Eyes Were Watching God;* she has already produced Gloria Naylor's *The Women of Brewster Place* and Toni Morrison's *Beloved.*

But Winfrey—remember, in this capitalist economy where sheer economic might renders the innately boorish Donald Trump a worthy newspaper or magazine cover, that Winfrey makes more than the Material Girl—did not make the cover of *People* magazine when her studio was built, or when she testified before Congress on sexual abuse of children (former Miss America Marilyn van Derbur had recently been on the cover discussing her own sexual abuse). She appeared on the cover when she announced, after a much-publicized liquid diet and subsequent weight regain,"I'll never diet again." In the context in which she probably wished to be read (if she wished to be read at all), that might mean, I am no longer going to worry about external standards of beauty, I am going to do what's best for my body and my emotional health. But the way it gets translated to a mainstream audience, and the only way to read the fact of the cover itself—remember, this is the same magazine that put Clarence Thomas and his wife on the cover following his Supreme Court confirmation hearings in an article in which Mrs. Thomas described those same hearings as "a battle between good and evil"—is that Oprah's audience can heave a collective sigh of relief because she will stay fat, therefore desexualized, therefore nonthreatening. The thin Oprah became an absurdity, as we saw in the Stallone quote and open media mockery of her Revlon advertisement in the early 1990s. How could mammy be one of the world's most unforgettable women? I felt palpable discomfort as I watched this spectacle, feeling it was only a matter of time before she'd gain back the weight on two hundred stations and in thirty-four foreign countries.

Think for a moment to the images of black women and food in a random sampling of television images with which each of us might be familiar. The company that produces Mrs. Butterworth's maple syrup may continue to insist, as they did when I wrote to them, that Mrs. Butterworth is "not intended to be of any specific ethnic origin," but her proximity to the pancake world, ample, rounded body, and the maple syrup-brown that in the clear plastic bottle becomes her skin color would suggest otherwise. The late Nell Carter in the popular sitcom *Gimme a Break* continually cooked and clowned for the white family that employed her; there is a bizarre absurdity to her discussing her weight problems with the bone-thin, compulsively weight-conscious Joan Rivers. With her later sitcom, Carter made a point of defusing the mammy stereotype by emphasizing that she and her black TV husband are sexually affectionate with each other. In another interesting update, on the black-produced *Cosby Show*, Claire and Cliff Huxtable spent comparable and considerable amounts of time in the kitchen cooking for their family, though Cliff's culinary forays were frequent comedic while Claire's were a more matter-of-fact dimension of her role in the family. It is Cliff who frets about his weight, sneaking hoagies and ice cream while the slinky Claire seems never to eat at all, yet it is also Cliff who is seen to derive profoundest emotional pleasure from eating. See, also, the *Fresh Prince of Bel Air* for interesting inversions of stereotypical roles of black women. Vivian's slim sexiness might be neutralized by her comically fat husband were it not for the insistent intimacy, sexual attraction, and familiarity between the two that is clear in the ways they play their roles.

Byllye Avery, founder of the National Black Women's Health Project, speaks frequently of her efforts to develop an approach to black women's health care that sees women's physical and emotional health as inextricably linked. She tells the story of a woman whose weight is a serious, continual threat to her health. She asks the woman why, if she knows how to diet, won't she try to lose weight. The woman tells about her life, about excruciatingly hard work for little compensation along with the demands of caring for her family. She says, to paraphrase: at the end of my day, I cook a big pot of food and sit in front of the TV and eat it, and I know how it's going to taste, and it tastes good, and it makes me feel good, and it's always there, and until I know something better, that's what I'm going to do. We wish for the health and satisfaction of this woman writ large. But her narrative is a starting point as it offers one account of a black woman's interior life and her relationship to food. What would it mean for Delilah to eat like she looks, to satiate herself like those she satiates? She is insatiable because there is no one to nourish her.

Betye Saar's painting *The Liberation of Aunt Jemima* shows the familiar Jemima icon with a semiautomatic weapon at the ready in place of the spatula, blasting away metaphorically at the confines of the imagery. Faith Ringgold's *One Hundred Pound Weight Loss Quilt* utilizes photographs of her large and shrinking body and a narration of her emotional associations with food and her body, literally in-corporating the black female forms of both quilting and food preparation with the iconographically invisible truths of emotional lives. Aunt Jemima herself has now been updated. The head-rag is gone, she's lost a bit of weight and wears a demure strand of pearls around her neck. The National Council of Negro Women led still by Dorothy Height has entered into a promotional agreement with the company, to update Jemima. But she is still "Aunt" Jemima, like her male counterpart "Uncle" Ben, "Aunt" and "Uncle" to the white children they nurture from their iconographic prisons.

Faith Ringgold's *Church Picnic Story Quilt* shows in great detail an epic spread of food prepared no doubt by black female hands. The blankets on which the food is spread in their variety invoke the black and female tradition of quilting. A written text around the quilted border narrates an afternoon in the life of a community and the ways in which food is an integral part of that. Sunday breakfast is cooked for "the ole folks"; a young woman just returned from missionary work in Africa doesn't feel like eating because her father has just died; a boy pesters his mother for yet another piece of chicken; stale wedding cake symbolizes a marriage for which no enthusiasm can be mustered, and so on. We need to consult black women's texts—oral, visual, sung, danced, and otherwise—to discern both the significance of food in our lives as well as the stories of our lives, rejecting as we have for so long, the notion that the fiction of a black female body says anything at all about who we really are.

I had to imagine that behind the flat, neon "Aunt Delilah" sign at the end of *Imitation of Life* were legions of black women at a Black Women's Health Project picnic, talking about their lives, plotting a hostile takeover of the Aunt Jemima corporation, and sharing gazpacho, fried chicken, buttered wheat rolls, linguine with pesto, green salad, black bean soup, bacalao with plantains, ceviche, macaroni and cheese, Yorkshire pudding, pigeon peas and rice, salmon cakes, sangria, and peach ice-cream. This is some of what we have been fed, some of what we feed each other, and one place that we can start to think about who we really are in these bodies of ours.

(1992)

Toni Cade's
The Black Woman: An Anthology

The year 1970 was an *annus mirabilis* for black women's writing. *The Bluest Eye* and *The Third Life of Grange Copeland* were first novels published by Toni Morrison and Alice Walker. Viking brought out *I Know Why the Caged Bird Sings,* the first of Maya Angelou's autobiographies.

"In the late '60s the publishing industry opened up in many ways," says Marie Dutton Brown, a literary agent and marketing consultant who has worked with a veritable pantheon of African-American literati and who, in the 1970s, was an associate editor at Doubleday. "Publishers and editors were more receptive, and of course we had the civil rights movement, and since it takes time for books to move through the contractual stage to publishing, by the time many of those books were done, it was 1970."

That same glittering year saw the publication of *The Black Woman: An Anthology,* edited by Toni Cade. She compiled this remarkable anthology before she had published her own books of fiction as Toni Cade Bambara *(The Salt-Eaters, Gorilla, My Love, The Sea Birds are Still Alive).* Twenty-three years later, the book is not only vibrant and instructive as far as nineties feminism goes, it is also still in print, a near-miracle for all but a few books by women and blacks.

In her introduction, Cade observed that "throughout the country in recent years, Black women have been forming work-study groups, discussion clubs, cooperative nurseries, cooperative businesses, consumer education groups, women's workshops on the campuses, women's caucuses within existing organizations, Afro-American women's magazines. . . . [T]hey have begun correspondence with sisters in Vietnam, Guatemala, Algeria, Ghana. . . . They are women who have not, it would seem, been duped by the prevailing notions of 'woman,' but who have maintained a critical stance" (9–10). This established *The Black Woman* not merely in response to assaults against black women's integrity but rather the outgrowth of work that had been ongoing.

The contributors are women who work in a range of fields, come of different experiences, and speak in different voices and genres. Frances Beale at the time was active in SNCC's Black Women's Liberation Committee. Carole Brown worked in antipoverty projects in California. Joanna Clark was an opera singer. Adele Jones was a member of the Black Student Alliance. Pat Robinson was a psychotherapist. The contributors who are best-known today mostly made their names as writers: Cade, Nikki Giovanni, Abbey Lincoln, Audre Lorde, Verta Mae Smart-Grosevenor, Paule Marshall, Shirley Williams (Sherley Anne Williams), and Alice Walker, whose contributor's note reads: "Stories have appeared in Black anthologies and in *Freedomways* magazine. New collection of stories being published. Formerly of Georgia, now resides in Mississippi."

The Black Woman is a post–Moynihan Report anthology that also works as a corrective to LeRoi Jones (Amiri Baraka) and Larry Neal's widely read 1968 anthology, *Black Fire,* which only included eight women in its roster of eighty-seven contributors, and, of course, to any number of feminist texts by white women in which the voices and experiences of black women were marginalized or not heard at all. *The Black Woman* was a crucial predecessor to black feminist landmark texts of the eighties such as *Midnight Birds and Black Eyed Susans, But Some of Us Are Brave,* and *Homegirls.* Today, there has not been another collection with aims as wide-ranging as these.

In an era of authorial singularity and something of an emergent star system for women writers, one of the most impressive aspects of *The Black Woman* is the way that many women's voices speak within the text. Luisah Teish uses the creole term *gumbo ya ya* to mean "everyone speaks at once" in black women's communities. A round-table discussion in *The Black Woman* emphasizes that, despite the title (and, really, what else might it have been called in 1970?), there is no one essential "black woman's experience" represented here. Cade dedicates the book, in the spirit of communality, to "the uptown mammas who nudged me to 'just set it down in print so it gets to be a habit to write letters to each other, so maybe that way we don't keep treadmilling the same ole ground'" (12).

The book moves from the condensed specificity of poetry, through the imagined world of fiction, to accounts of living women's lives, to more programmatic essays. Sometimes those lines are blurred within individual pieces, such as Joanna Clark's "Motherhood," which opens with, "My first words as I came from under the ether after I had my son were, 'I think I made a mistake'" (63) and ends with, "As mothers, we are worse off than we think we are. In the age of the sit-in and the be-in, it is time for a sit-down and let's not get up off of it until there's at least social security and employment insurance for every mother" (72).

I've read and reread this book so many times that I don't remember when the first time was. To say I've read it implies that I've moved straight through, but what I love about anthologies is that they invite readers to pick and choose as their lives allow. It wasn't until I recently taught the book to a group of graduate students and upper-level undergraduates in a course on contemporary African-American literature that I had an opportunity to think again about the sum-total effect of this book. It worked remarkably well with my students, who found it addressed contemporary concerns in both the class and their lives.

When I read this book in college in the early eighties, what I needed from black women's writing was almost a roll call, numbers, company. Any voice that fell under the moniker *black woman* was mine, and I adapted to that perspective, trying (unsuccessfully) to ease my way through what we now call "difference" in the name of "sisterhood."

Today, *The Black Woman* makes me think hard about the ways in which my experiences and goals do and don't intersect with those of the multitude of women whom I might call "sister." Black women have been divided among lines of color, class, sexuality, and so much else. What I take from *The Black Woman*, and what I think was resonant for my students, as well, is the notion, as Cade says in the book, that "[e]ach of us, after all, has particular skills and styles that suit us for particular tasks in the struggle. I'm not altogether sure we agree on the phrase 'revolution' or I wouldn't be having so much difficulty with the phrase 'woman's role'" (101). The understanding is always hard-won that moving forward as a group is less about simple celebration and smoothing over differences than it is about finding a way to follow the dictum of Audre Lorde and so many others that we must acknowledge and then utilize our differences.

Still, I insist that there is a need and a use for a book called *The Black Woman*, there are bottom-line moments marked by race and gender, and there is call for celebration. That's when I like to read someone like Verta Mae Smart-Grosevenor in *The Black Woman*, being wise about food and life:

> so called enlightened people will rap for hours about jean paul sartre, campus unrest, the feminine mystique, black power, and tania, but mention food and they say, rather proudly, too, "i'm a bad cook." some go as far to boast "i can't even boil water without burning it."
> that is a damn shame.
> bad cooks got a bad life style
> food is life
> . . .
> PROTECT YOUR KITCHEN.
>
> (121–23)

The last essay in *The Black Woman* is "Are the Revolutionary Techniques Employed in the Battle of Algiers Applicable to Harlem." The book helps to articulate the many contours of what constitutes revolution, both in 1970 and today. Its dust jacket trumpets, "[T]oday America is witnessing two great human revolutions. One is that of burgeoning black pride and militancy. The other is the rising demand by women for liberation from their chattel-like roles in a male-dominated society. This volume presents the eloquent writings of those vitally involved in both—Black women, speaking of and for themselves."

In addition to being a year of symbolic wonders for black women's writing, 1970 was also the year that two black students were shot and killed by police at Jackson State University, and the year that Angela Davis was arrested. Today, black women "speaking of and for themselves" is still, as it has been historically, an act of, if not outright revolution, nonetheless resistance to a repressive status quo. It has always been so. But Cade's words in 1970 clarify my thinking of what it means to try to live in an aware, committed, and righteous way:

"Revolution begins with the self, in the self. The individual, the basic revolutionary unit, must be purged of poison and lies that assault the ego and threaten the heart, that hazard the next larger unit—the family or cell, that puts the entire movement in peril. . . . If your house ain't in order, you ain't in order" (109–10). As editor and contributor, she reminds me that self-change and world change takes commitment and the necessity for struggle.

An all of that, in paperback, for $3.95.

(1991)

"Coming Out Blackened and Whole"

Fragmentation and Reintegration in Audre Lorde's Zami *and* The Cancer Journals

1.

"As a Black woman," said the late Audre Lorde, "I have to deal with identity or I don't exist at all. I can't depend on the world to name me kindly, because it never will. If the world defines you, it will define you to your disadvantage. So either I'm going to be defined by myself or not at all."[1] In essays from her *Sister Outsider* and *A Burst of Light* as well as in the more narratively autobiographical *Zami: A New Spelling of My Name* and *The Cancer Journals,* Lorde names differences among women, African-Americans, lesbians, and other groups as empowering rather than divisive forces and as aspects of identity. The political ideal, as she sees it, should not be a melting pot where all difference is subsumed, usually bending to the descriptive and ideological might of the previously dominant group. Instead, Lorde argues, difference within the self is a strength to be called upon rather than a liability to be altered. She exhorts her readers to recognize how each of them is multifarious and need never choose one aspect of identity at the expense of the others. "There's always someone asking you to underline one piece of yourself," she said in a 1981 interview,

> whether it's *Black, woman, mother, dyke, teacher,* etc.—because that's the piece that they need to key in to. They want you to dismiss everything else. But once you do that, then you've lost because then you become acquired or bought by that partic-ular essence of yourself, and you've denied yourself all of the

energy that it takes to keep all those others in jail. Only by learning to live in harmony with your contradictions can you keep it all afloat. . . . That's what our work comes down to. No matter where we key into it, it's the same work, just different pieces of ourselves doing it.[2]

Each of us, says Lorde, needs each of those myriad pieces to make us who we are and whole. Lorde works the science and logic of her own hybridity. "I had never been too good at keeping within straight lines, no matter what their width," she writes in *Zami*.[3] She must make a physical space for herself in a hybrid language, a composite, a creation of new language to make space for the "new" of the self-invented body.

The implications of this thinking for questions of identity are broad. For the self to remain simultaneously multiple and integrated, embracing the definitive boundaries of each category—race, gender, class, et cetera—while dissembling their static limitations, assumes a depth and complexity of identity construction that refutes a history of limitation. For the self to be fundamentally collaged—overlapping and discernibly dialogic— is to break free from diminishing concepts of identity. Lorde says, "When I say myself, I mean not only the Audre who inhabits my body but all those feisty, incorrigible black women who insist on standing up and saying '*I am* and you cannot wipe me out, no matter how irritating I am, how much you fear what I might represent.'"[4] The self is comprised of multiple components within the self and evolved from multiple external sources, an African-American women's tradition or mythos.

The Cancer Journals is Lorde's memoir of her battle with the disease, but the scope of the meditation, as well as Lorde's formal freedom, makes it much more. For *Zami* she has invented a name for the book's new, collaged genre: *biomythography*. Neither autobiography, biography, nor mythology, biomythography is all of those things and none of them, a collaged space in which useful properties of genres are borrowed and reconfigured according to how well they help tell the story of a particular African-American woman's life. *Biomythography* both refers to each of its eponymous genres and defines itself in its present moment.

I will consider how in this biomythographic mode Lorde's vision of collaged self-construction is mirrored in her compositional choices. With *biomythography* Lorde names a new genre, creating a larger space for her myriad selves. "I feel that not to be open about any of the different 'people' within my identity," she said in an interview, "particularly the 'mes' who are challenged by a status quo, is to invite myself and other women, by my example, to live a lie. In other words, I would be giving in to a myth of sameness which I think can destroy us."[5]

Both *Zami* and *The Cancer Journals* favor nonlinear narration that plays with chronology as it needs to. Both are autobiographies of Lorde's body. Both books are also erotic autobiographies, with *Zami* in particular describing Lorde's sensual life in intricate detail. The African-American woman's body in Lorde's work—specifically, her own body—becomes a map of lived experience and a way of printing suffering as well as joy upon the flesh. Because the history of the black female sexual body is fraught with lies and distortion, the story of those bodies as told by their inhabiters must take place on new, self-charted terrain with the marks of a traumatic history like a palimpsest. Like Carriacou, the Caribbean home of Lorde's antecedents that she as a child could not find on any map at school, the body of flesh or land that does not accurately exist in white American eyes leaves the inhabitant open for self-invention and interpretation. The flesh, the text, remains scarred, marking the trail to self-creation.

Lorde is preoccupied with things bodily: that which is performed upon the body versus what the body performs and asserts. Cancer surgery and subsequent bodily struggles are the focus of *The Cancer Journals*, while the ingestion of X-ray crystals at a factory job and an illegal abortion are signal episodes in *Zami*. Sexual and spiritual woman-love are what the body performs and how it heals, as well as the means by which Lorde finds voice and self-expression. She in-corporates the intellectual and physical aspects of her life, reminding the reader that the metaphysical resides in a physical space, the body. Thus rage and oppression are metabolized to cancer, but she will also "write fire until it comes out of my eras, my eyes, my noseholes—everywhere. Until it's every breath I breathe."[6] In Lorde's work, the body speaks its own history; she chooses corporeal language to articulate what she could not previously put into words.

In *The Cancer Journals,* for instance, Lorde dreams of a different vocabulary for considering this phenomenon. She recounts a dream in which "I had begun training to change my life" and she follows a "shadowy teacher":

> Another young woman who was there told me she was taking a course in "language crazure," the opposite of discrazure (the cracking and wearing away of rock). I thought it would be very exciting to study the formation and crack and composure of words, so I told my teacher I wanted to take that course. My teacher said okay, but it wasn't going to help me any because I had to learn something else, and I wouldn't get anything new from that class. I replied maybe not, but even though I knew all about rocks, for instance, I still liked studying their composition, and giving a name to the different ingredients of which they were made. It's very exciting to think of me being all the people in this dream.[7]

"[T]he formation and crack and composure" of words mirrors the process of reconstituting the scarred self. Lorde thinks of herself as all of the people in the dream. She is at once the self who wants to learn about language, the self who explores new selves and ideas, the censorial teacher-self as well as the self who gives permission for new exploration, albeit grudgingly. The dream allows for the simultaneous existence of different selves coexisting as a single self, and the contemplation of form, crack, and composure mirrors how the self is continually brought back together from disassembled fragments. Perhaps she is playing also, in the way that dreams play tricks with language, with the words *crazure* and *discrazure,* with first being considered "crazy," as Lorde tells us she has been since elementary school, and then coming to see the roots of *craze* as, in fact, whole and sane. In *crazure* the lines and fissures are visible, but the object—like Lorde herself—remains whole.

In *Zami* Lorde describes the process of constructing herself racially and sexually with race and gender both facts of biology and learned characteristics and social operatives. To be "blackened" reveals not only a process of becoming and being acted upon but also a state of being. Lorde restores the visual impact of "coming out" to suggest her assertion and arrival and also, of course, playing on lesbian "coming out." Hers is a process of becoming black and lesbian on her own terms as much as it is being named and seen as those things by a larger world. "Blackened" is a positive state to "come out" into, but it also implies being burnt and scarred. The statement's ending—"and whole"—suggests no contradiction between being scarred and being whole (*Zami* 5). In Lorde's work, life experience ever marks and takes shape as visible body memory, as a collage whose assembled scraps always allude to their past and beyond to a collective race memory of the violence of rupture in the Middle Passage, as encoded by the African-American collage artist Romare Bearden. When Lorde refers to the "journeywoman pieces of myself" (*Zami* 5), she configures the self as simultaneously fragmented and reassembled.

Zami's first section is an unlabeled preprologue, a dedication of sorts in which Lorde asks questions in italics and then muses upon them in roman typeface. This introduces us to the dialogism of Lorde's work, in which process is always apparent and the self is presented as an unfinished work in transition and progress. Collage, too, is dialogic at its core, insofar as the cut and torn strips encode a dialogue between past and ever evolving present. That referentiality of using a scrap that on closer scrutiny can be identified both with its former life and as part of the present fiction recalls Bearden's earlier work, in which pieces were readily associated with their origins. Interestingly, Bearden later works continually with origami-like paper in ways less obviously allusive to a separate past than his earlier newspaper and magazine cutouts.[8] This gesture reflects the assurance of both self and voice in Bearden's mature work. By engaging visibly in the dialogic aspects of collage, *Zami* ruminates on how the self is put together and how the book is the body for Lorde's ideas about self-construction.

2.

Images of black people's bodies in American culture have been either hypersexualized or desexualized to serve the imaginings and purposes of white American men and women. African-American men have been iconographically exploited as either black buck (in the nineteenth century, renegade slave; in the twentieth, athlete or criminal) or docile, smiling eunuch (in the nineteenth century, men seen as "Uncles"—Remus, or Jim in the river raft, without children of their own and without discernible sexuality—in the twentieth century, obsequious entertainers). Black women, similarly, have been iconographically exploited as the hypersexualized Jezebel who entices the supposedly unrapacious master into her pallet or as the desexualized mammy who has no children or loves her white "babies" as her own. Her body is very much a part of her image: as mammy she is a comforting void of avoirdupois, while the Jezebel's curvaceous body is prominently displayed like an emblem of her social status or her essence. It is startling how, even today, there is so little iconographic gray space with these images. Historian Gerda Lerner writes that the postslavery mythology of blacks was created to maintain social control. She specifically addresses the mythicizing of black women's sexual freedom and abandon so that they were seen as women who

> therefore, deserved none of the consideration and respect granted to white women. Every black woman was, by definition, a slut according to this racist mythology; therefore, to assault her and explicit her sexually was not reprehensible and carried with it none of the normal communal sanctions against such behavior. A wide range of practices reinforced this myth: the laws against intermarriage; the denial of the title "Miss" or "Mrs." to any black woman; the taboos against respectable social mixing of the races; the refusal to let black women customers try on clothing in stores before making a purchase; the assigning of single toilet facilities to both sexes of Blacks; the different legal sanctions against rape, abuse of minors and other sex crimes when committed against white or black women. Black women were very much aware of the interrelatedness of these practices and fought constantly—individually and through their organizations—both the practices and the underlying myth.[9]

This continual need to prove oneself sexually respectable—as if one ever could—against such a backdrop of accusation and assumption made the frank discussion of one's own sexuality dangerous. The need to name oneself, rather than leave it to a hostile dominant culture, is shown in the way in *Zami* Lorde and her late-teenaged friends call themselves "The Branded": "We became The Branded because we learned how to make a virtue out of it" (82).

Lorde's mapping of her body is all the more powerful against this history, as is her reclaiming and redefining of the erotic in her groundbreaking essay "Uses of the Erotic: The Erotic as Power":

> The erotic has often been misnamed by men and used against women. It has been made into the confused, the trivial, the psychotic, the plasticized sensation. For this reason, we have often turned away from the exploration and consideration of the erotic as a source of power and information, confusing it with its opposite, the pornographic. But pornography is a direct denial of the power of the erotic, for it represents the suppression of true feeling. Pornography emphasizes sensation without feeling.[10]

Lorde carefully separates eroticism from abuse of sexuality, freeing herself and those who would write after her from the idea that black women's sexuality is to be whispered about and to be ashamed of. She reminds us that "[t]he very word *erotic* comes from the Greek word *eros,* the personification of love in all its aspects—born of Chaos, and personifying creative power and harmony. When I speak of the erotic, then, I speak of it as an assertion of the life force of women; of that creative energy empowered, the knowledge and use of which we are now reclaiming in our language, our history, our dancing, our loving, our work, our lives" (55). Eroticism as she defines it has nothing at all to do with how African-American women are conventionally sexualized.

Lorde keeps readers aware of what the body feels, piece by piece, throughout the narratives. We are always aware of what her body is doing and feeling, from abortion cramps to sweat running between her breasts at 3:00 a.m. (*Zami* 117). This is in contrast to her mother's "euphemisms of body": "bamsy," "lower region," "between your [not 'my'] legs," all "whispered" (*Zami*

32). Further, Lorde talks about the body as a thing put together and taken apart. In both *The Cancer Journals* and *Zami* she isolates the breast and its symbolic meaning for motherhood and heterosexual beauty and then reconceives her own body by talking about what the breast means to her: yes, it gives her pleasure, but not apart from the rest of her body. The female breast can be prosthetically replaced, but Lorde needs to create and articulate her own grammar of physical significance.

Lorde continually refers to her physical self; phrases such as "when I was five years old and still legally blind" (*Zami* 21) give the reader a corporeal landmark in her life's chronology, calling attention again to the conflict black women frequently experience between public authority and self-authority. She is blind in the eyes of the law, yet she has already given us accounts of what she sees around her. We have before us, then, a legally blind narrative we have nonetheless come to trust. The emphasis on legality in "legally blind" calls up the ironies of legal and extralegal categories in African-American life: "chattel personal" defined full human beings, and so on. Lorde points to a distrust of the American common legal system and asks readers instead to trust her authority as she recounts the details she remembers seeing. Young Audre enters a "sight conservation class" but shows us a "blue wooden booth," "white women," "milk," "black mother," and "red and white tops" (*Zami* 21). It turns out that the seven or eight black children in her class all have "serious deficiencies of sight"; are all these children wrong and legally deficient? Lorde's authority supersedes legal status and public logic.

Lorde yokes the physical and conceptual when she recalls a doctor who "clip[ped] the little membrane under my tongue so I was no longer tongue-tied" (*Zami* 23). To be tongue-tied is to have an encumbered, surgically correctable tongue as well as to be at a loss for words or without language, and Lorde literalizes this metaphorized tongue: she gives a physical home and tangible, corporeal image to the concept of self-expression. The tongue, the physical organ that enables speech, is clipped that she might speak, and Lorde mines that act of surgical violence, of bodily invasion, to talk about speaking, expression, re-creation, and acting. Similarly, when struggling for money, Lorde sells her blood for plasma. Blood is a synecdoche for the surviving body and its sale a metaphor for the idea of "living off of her body." That is, she sells a regenerative part so the whole can live.

Moreover, blood "belongs" inside of the body, but Lorde externalizes it, as she constantly turns her body inside out, showing us the hidden insides that amplify how the outside has been maligned and distorted; the metaphysical inside is never known unless she chooses to reveal it. Conversely, the X-ray crystals that Lorde counts in the factory are brought inside the body in another inversion of nature. She buries them deeper and deeper in her body, first secreting them in her thick socks, then taking them into her mouth, chewing them up and imbibing some part of them even as they are spit out in the bathroom.

Lorde's photograph makes up the full front cover of the first edition of *The Cancer Journals*. Here she makes herself, her body, empirical, the best evidence of her arguments and self-definitions. She illustrates that she is all she proclaims herself to be—fat and black and beautiful—but that cover is also a strange testament to her very physical existence: she is a survivor and alive. She shows us the inside of her body to gain a kind of documentary, empirical self-referencing, authority as an expert on her own life and as the maker of a life on paper. For neither that life, her own, nor that of any black woman, has ever existed in representation as its possessor experienced it. Consider the case of the Hottentot Venus, a southern African woman named Saartje Baartman (tribal name unknown) brought to Europe in the early nineteenth century under the impression that she was to earn money that she could take back to her family.[11] Instead, she was exhibited nude in circuses and private balls in London and Paris; eager Europeans paid to see her steatophygia. A French scientist, George Cuvier, made a name for himself by performing experiments of an unspecified nature upon her body and by dissecting her buttocks and genitalia after her death at the age of twenty-five. Baartman came to signify sexual and racial difference represented in extremis, as well as the attitude that black women's bodies were easily commodified and utterly dispensable. Baartman's case represents as well another side of the exploitation of black women: the burning desire to see further and further inside, to have access to every crack and crevice of a black woman's body and to that which she has tried to keep sacred. This underlines the power of Lorde showing us her insides, that sanctified, veiled territory that looks so different because she is showing it herself.

3.

Zami's subtitle, "a new spelling of my name," hints that the alphabet—shapes that when put together make discernible meaning—will be rearranged. The "me" or "my" that name represents remains constant: Audre Lorde, as we her readers know her. But the moniker is what is new and what will unfold in the book; what the self is called and what it calls itself are not necessarily identical things. The theme of naming and renaming oneself is familiar within African-American culture, of course. Instead of the example of Malcolm X, whose *X* stands as a sign of empty space, negation and refutation of the white patriarch's legacy, Lorde respells her name altogether. She empties language, even letters, of previous signifiers as she plays with these received symbols. Lorde makes use of all that is available to her, just as African-American experience incorporates the joy of transported and reassembled culture as it remembers the ugly rupture of the Middle Passage. Lorde works with that same alphabet to make a newly named and new self altogether. *Spelling* works both as a noun (how the word is spelled) as well as an active verb form (the process of spelling). So Lorde engages in spelling and reinventing, a work in progress who has not necessarily settled at a fixed meaning or identity. "A" new spelling (as opposed to "the") means there is probably more to come.

The way Lorde sees before she gets glasses and the validity of that vision challenges conventional ways of seeing and knowing. The first story she writes as a child, Lorde tells us, is a collage as well as a rebus: "I like White Rose Salada tea" (*Zami* 29), with the rose represented by a picture clipped from the *New York Times Magazine* and by letters spelling her story. "How I Became a Poet" (*Zami* 31–34) challenges the concept of chapters.

Unattributed quotations challenge the notion of authorship and attribution.

"Growing up Fat Black Female and almost blind in america requires so much surviving that you have to learn from it or die," Lorde writes in *The Cancer Journals* (40). She spells America with a lowercase *a,* again exercising her prerogative as maker of the body of the book and letting her spelled language bear her perspective on the world. She chooses not to capitalize the name of a country that she sees as "cold and raucous" (*Zami* 11). Carriacou is her ancestral home, but the body of the country, the physical spot, while not locatable in any official text (the map), is utterly integral to her sense of self and ancestry. "Once *home* was a far way off, a place I had never been to but knew well out of my mother's mouth" (*Zami* 13), she continues. If a body of land does not even appear on a paper map but incontrovertibly exists, emitted from her mother's actual body, she must trust her own authority and be utterly free to experience and know it according to an internal family barometer. Invisibility, rather than distorted visibility, ironically provides a higher degree of self-inventive freedom.

Harlem is capitalized, while *america* is not; Lorde gives herself that authority of capitalization. For upper- and lowercase letters imply caste or class, both suggested and contained within *case.* Lorde plays with the spelling of her name from the beginning of the biomythography, describing her decision to drop the *y* on her birth name Audrey for love of the solidity and visual symmetry of Audre Lorde:

> I did not like the tail of the Y hanging down below the line in Audrey, and would always forget to put it on, which used to disturb my mother greatly. I used to love the evenness of AUDRELORDE at four years of age, but I remembered to put on the Y because it pleased my mother, and because, as she always insisted to me, that was the way it had to be because that was the way it was. No deviation was allowed from her interpretations of correct. (*Zami* 24)

Lorde echoes this theme in *The Cancer Journals.* Discussing the politics of prostheses, she talks about carving one's physical self to someone else's idea of correctness rather than to one's own sense of symmetry. That dangling Y is in a way like a prosthetic limb or breast: once the new and natural shape of the body is to have one breast, just as the new and natural shape of the name is the indeed wonderfully even AUDRELORDE, addenda are prosthetic, unnecessary, and in their way de-forming.

Later, young Audre writes her name at school in what she thinks is her most glorious penmanship, moving slantwise down the page in another kind of symmetry. She works hard at this display, "half-showing off, half-eager to please" (*Zami* 25). She wants to write with pencil, which is how she has learned and the way she thinks is proper, but is given a crayon instead. Crayon, we are to think, is much coarser and less exact than the sharp pencil, for children and not for adults. Lorde makes do, but her teacher says, "I see we have a young lady who does not want to do as she is told" (26). This moment in which the narrator's "right" is presented in opposition to a public "right" is an important trope in black women's autobiography; without resistance, survival and growth are impossible in an unjust world. Since we have been set up to identify with the narrator, as readers we align ourselves against the tyrannical dominant culture and with the contested genius of the black girl-child. This is how we learn the lesson that to follow instructions, to play by what you think are the rules, does not always garner the expected perquisites.

In that instance of childhood we see Lorde asserting her own way of *writing*—not yet "spelling" explicitly, as the title would indicate, but spelling in the fundamental way that a child spells when every act of writing is a conscious act of putting together the pieces that make words that then hold meaning. To spell one's name is to create oneself in language, in Lorde's words, to put together "all the journeywoman pieces of myself" into one's most public signifier: the name.

Also present in *Zami* is the signal scene in African-American autobiography in which the slave learns to read and to transcend a received legal status, thus entering the domain in which literacy is experienced as freedom. Lorde learns to read and speak simultaneously "because of [her] nearsightedness," distilling from apparent deficiency a new way of learning. Describing this, Lorde establishes a firm link between literacy and self-expression:

> I took the books from Mrs. Baker's hands after she was finished reading, and traced the large black letters with my fingers, while I peered again at the beautiful bright colors of the pictures. Right then I decided I was going to find out how to do that myself. I pointed to the black marks which I could now distinguish as separate letters, different from my sisters' more grown-up books, whose smaller print made the pages only one gray blur for me. I said, quite loudly, for whoever was listening to hear, "I want to read." (23)

This scene demonstrates Lorde's understanding that letters and words have physicality, that language has a body, and that the physical place in which communicated language resides is important. This leads the reader, herself engaged in an act of literacy as she reads the book, to reexperience that lost sense of the word's physicality. After this scene, Lorde's mother teaches her "to say the alphabet forwards and backward as it was done in Grenada" (23). Lorde's logic, bodily and intellectual, finds sense in the so-called backward as well as in the forwards.

Lorde describes her mother as follows: "My mother was a very powerful woman. This was so in a time when that word-combination of *woman* and *powerful* was almost unexpressable in the white american common tongue, except or unless it was accompanied by some aberrant explaining adjective like blind, or hunchback, or crazy, or Black" (*Zami* 15). For her mother to exist in language as she knows her, Lorde must trust her own knowledge and her own developing linguistic cosmos. She must also become attuned to what she knows outside of spoken language. She says that "my mother must have been *other* than woman" (16) because of her authority, because of the way she did not fit what "the white american common tongue" would represent as "Black and foreign and female in New York City in the twenties" (17). Lorde writes, "It was so often her approach to the world; to change reality. If you can't change reality, change your perceptions of it" (18). Lorde's mother in some regards provided a blueprint for Lorde's ability to change form to suit her needs, to change an outside perception of her body by inserting her own sense of form, both literary and physical. In an interview with Adrienne Rich, Lorde said she learned from her mother "[t]he important value of nonverbal communication, beneath language. My life depended on it. . . . . eventually I learned how to acquire vital and protective information without words. My mother used to say to me, 'Don't just listen like a ninny to what people say in their mouth.'"[12] Language makes space for self-articulation and allows the self-invented body to name itself and to exist. Like so many other African-American women writers, Lorde must make a physical space for herself in a hybrid and composite language wherein what she knows is frequently at odds with what the world tells her she should see.

4.

On a family trip to Washington, D.C., Lorde describes the agony of what her eyes actually see. The trip marks the hardest smack with direct racism and segregation that the family had experienced and takes place "on the edge of the summer when I was supposed to stop being a child" (*Zami* 68). Great preparation is made in the family for the trip; food is cooked and packed for the train along with suitcases. Lorde sees everything there "through an agonizing corolla of dazzling white-ness" (69) which at the same time dazzles and blinds. The color of Washington's buildings represents who runs them; it is beautiful, what the family members have come to see, but it is also what they are up against and what they are not, for when they stop on the hot summer day for vanilla ice cream (more blinding whiteness) they are not allowed to eat at the counter. Washington is "real" and "official" as a site of power, and Lorde, on the brink of a new maturity, sees what is painful in the white dazzle: "The waitress was white, and the counter was white, and the ice cream I never ate in Washington, D.C. that summer I left childhood was white, and the white heat and the white pavement and the white stone monuments of my first Washington summer made me sick to my stomach for the whole rest of that trip" (71). Here we see a direct example, as well, of how her body absorbs and metabolizes her life's experiences, including painful ones. Her body holds and manifests that which has happened to her psyche. She develops a long-lasting stomachache from the moment she is acted upon via the seeing power of her eyes, as though the white is a tincture of evil.

Lorde writes of the "secret fears which allow cancer to flourish" (*Cancer* 10). In both books taken together, cancer is inescapably a metaphor for the dangers of growing up poor, female, and black. She metabolizes the fears that others have of her, from teachers to exploitative employers. The episode where she describes her abortion and the episode when she works in Keystone Electronics most vividly illustrate this.

The abortion segment is graphic, necessarily. "Now all I had to do was hurt" (*Zami* 110), she writes, after she has had the catheter inserted into her uterus. This both isolates and delays bodily experience. The rubber eventually works its way out, as does the fetus. She keeps the reader ever aware of exactly how she is feeling; "[T]his action which was tearing my guts apart and from which I could die except I wasn't going to—this action was a kind of shift from safety towards self-preservation. It was a choice of pains. That's what living was all about" (*Zami* 111). The fetus is, of course, a part of her body as it grows inside of her, but it is a part that she wants to be rid of. To get rid of the life-burden of an unwanted child she must have this physical symbol of that invasion removed. Like a tumor, a fetus grows unwittingly.

Lorde has worked in two doctor's offices but cannot type and is young, poor, female, and black, so she ends up working in a factory that processes X-ray crystals used in radio and radar machinery. The place was "offensive to every sense, too cold and too hot, gritty, noisy, ugly, sticky, stinking, and dangerous" (*Zami* 126). She counts X-ray crystals with black and Puerto Rican women whose fingers are permanently darkened from exposure to the radiation: "Nobody mentioned that carbon tet destroys the liver and causes cancer of the kidneys. Nobody mentioned that the X-ray machines, when used unshielded, delivered doses of constant low radiation far in excess of what was considered safe even in those days" (*Zami* 126).

Workers could earn bonuses for "reading" crystals past a certain amount, but the factory bosses scrutinized them, making sure they did not discard crystals and claim credit for them. Lorde, in need of money, figures out a way to beat the system. She slips crystals into her socks every time she goes to the bathroom, and once inside the stall, "I chewed them up with my strong teeth and flushed the little shards of rock down the commode. I could take care of between fifty and a hundred crystals a day in that manner, taking a handful from each box I signed out" (*Zami* 146). She chews the crystals and spits them out; they are nonfood but nonetheless "metabolized"; as she tells us hatred, too, can be metabolized. The body, then, makes visible also what has been metaphorically imbibed. Lorde's cancer turns the body inside out, alluding to the internal lacerations of chewed X-ray crystals, which are themselves a manifestation of what a poor black female has to do to survive. Lorde earns unprecedented amounts of money—for the factory, of course—and is laid off shortly thereafter. The X-ray crystals have stained her fingertips, leaving her marked with the work of her class status and with the illness she will eventually develop. She says she has a sense of the fingers burning off (*Zami* 146). A reader of *The Cancer Journals* cannot escape the conclusion that this episode contributed largely to her subsequent illness.

By insistently reminding the reader of her bodily reality, Lorde works toward the body's integration through struggle, a synecdoche for the struggle of the self to remain whole. The women she admires are whole in their variegated bodies. One of the first images she presents of a woman outside of her family is of a woman named DeLois who walks on the street, her "big proud stomach" (*Zami* 4) attracting sunlight. She tells of one of her early, significant love affairs, in Mexico, with a woman, Eudora (*Zami* 161–76), who had had breast cancer—eerily presaging the future of Lorde's own healing, whole-ing process, just as it is "the love of women," though not explicitly erotic love, that heals her in *The Cancer Journals*. Making love, how the body acts, is a counterpart or an antidote to what has been done to it. Making love (the erotic) as a creative act (as power) is a self-making and self-defining act. Even autoerotic love, masturbation, is written about as a part of the process of healing the body and making it and the resident psyche whole again (*Cancer* 40).

5.

Lorde survives despite "grow[ing] up fat, Black, nearly blind, and ambidextrous in a West Indian household" (*Zami* 24). "Ambidextrous" plays on the fact that she tells us about sleeping with both men and women, but it also deals more seriously with the notion of self-creation and incorporating power. To be ambidextrous, then, is another instance of bodily states, facts of nature, existing as metaphors for aspects of identity. She talks about her mother as being both, other, and says that she, too, wishes for ambidextrous self-culled sexual identity: *"I have always wanted to be both man and women, to incorporate the strongest and richest parts of my mother and father within/into me. . . . I have felt the age-old triangle of mother father and child, with the 'I' at its eternal core, elongate and flatten out into the elegantly strong triad of grandmother mother daughter, with the 'I' moving back and forth flowing in either or both directions as needed"* (7). Identity is fluid, as is demonstrated by the elision of punctuation in *"mother father and child"* and *"grandmother mother daughter."*

The essay "A Burst of Light" serves as a postscript to *The Cancer Journals,* synthesizing and further distilling many of its ideas. Lorde makes explicit connections between becoming an authority on one's own body and cancer and politics, dying and struggling to live and work. Much of the essay is an exhausting chronicle of the work she keeps up with around the globe as she is fighting the disease; a refrain is "I [or 'we,' with her lover, Frances] did good work." She fights experts and decides she does not want the borders of her body to be invaded. She rejects medical advice when it is her life at stake. When she says she wants to have "[e]nough moxie to chew the whole world up and spit it out in bite-sized pieces, useful and warm and wet and delectable because they came out of my mouth" (62), the image recalls and inverts the chewed and spit out X-ray crystals. *To metabolize* means to take in good and bad and then determine what is useful in the shaping of the self. The act that probably poisoned her can be reenacted to her advantage.

Lorde travels to a holistic healing center and finds a philosophy wherein "the treatment of any disease, and cancer in particular, must be all of a piece, body and mind, and I am ready to try anything so long as they don't come at me with a knife" (83). Divisibility and invasion are worse even than cancer.

She rejects a prosthesis in part because the breast does not "perform," as a leg or an arm does. She realizes it is not its own erotic world, not erotic unto itself, but rather part of a schema of eros she controls and that is integral within her body. She explores what the body performs versus what is done to the body: abortion, cancer surgery. Body language is a necessary part of naming herself in her own tongue.

Lorde's work, as it focuses on her physical existence, emphasizes the literal meaning of incorporation, of putting one's self into a body, or in this case, speaking of one's self in one's own body. The intellect lives and operates in the body. The heart and soul express themselves through the body. the body manifests the ills of an oppressive world that is especially punishing to women and poor people and people of color. The body is a very specific site in Lorde's work, the location where all this takes place. She is constantly reminding us that she is an inhabitant of a body that has given birth to children, been nearly blind, and has battled cancer and lost pieces of itself but remains whole, incorporated, integrated. It is *"[m]y body, a living representation of other life older longer wiser"* (*Zami* 7). Bodies express what verbal language cannot.

6.

> I am a scar, a report from the frontlines, a talisman, a resurrection.
> —Audre Lorde, "A Burst of Light: Living with Cancer"

In James Alan McPherson's "The Story of a Scar," the African-American male protagonist sits in a plastic surgeon's waiting room and from the first page is compelled to ask the African-American woman next to him, "As a concerned person, and as your brother, I ask you, without meaning to offend, how did you get that scar on the side of your face?"[13] She rebuffs his bold inquiry and his presumption that she will "read" her own body for him. "'I ask *you*,' she said, 'as a nosy person with no connections in your family, how come your nose is all bandaged up?'" (97). His bandaged nose makes his nosiness legible. As the story proceeds from the man's narrative perspective, the woman tells her story, only to be continually interrupted by the man's presumptions about her narrative. He presumes to know her and to know what the mark on her face signifies. He presumes he has access to that signification because, after all, the mark is visible, and if a black woman's body is visible, it is therefore accessible, not only to white men, historically, but in this instance for black men as well.

But she will not let him get away with that and will not let her story be usurped. She "reads" him as well. "'You don't have to tell me a thing,' she said. 'I know mens goin' and comin'. There ain't a-one of you I'd trust to take my grandmama to Sunday school'" (98). The male protagonist persists:

> The scar still fascinated me. . . . The scar was thick and black and crosscrossed with a network of old stitch patterns, as if some meticulous madman had first attempted to carve a perfect half-circle in her flesh, and then decided to embellish his handiwork. It was so grotesque a mark that one had the feeling it was the art of no human hand and could be peeled off like so much soiled putty. But this was a surgeon's office and the scar was real. It was as real as the honey-blond wig she wore, as real as her purple pantsuit. I studied her approvingly. She women have a natural leaning toward the abstract expression of themselves. Their styles have private meanings, advertise secret distillations of their souls. Their figures, and their disfigurations, make meaningful statements. (98–99)

As it turns out, the woman has been marked by public violence by a man. Her scar is a history of sorts, a mark she is trying to change. The more she tells of her story the more she gives away of herself, leaving both of them on uncertain ground, but she will not simply cut to the chase and tell the *mere* "story of a scar"; she is telling a piece of her life, telling the story her way regardless of how the listener wants to receive it. The man characterizes her story as "tiresome ramblings," and she becomes angry: "This here's *my* story! . . . You dudes cain't stand to hear the whole of anything. You want everything broke down in little pieces. . . . That's how come you got your nose all busted up. There's some things you have to take your time about" (100).

When she finishes her story, her talk is not interrupted narratively for several pages; she takes over the narrative space of the story with her bodily truth. The male narrator then interrupts and gives a condescending and erroneous conclusion to her story (105). She then takes the space of a long pause and a dramatic drag on her cigarette. "'You know everything,' she said in a soft tone, much unlike her own. 'A black mama birthed you, let you suck her titty, cleaned your dirty drawers, and you still look at us through paper and movie plots'" (105–6).

After the story is finished, after he has had to listen to her truth, a "terrifying fog of silence and sickness crept into the small room, and there was no longer the smell of medicine" (111). There are no longer antidotes, only dis-ease, the fact of the scar and the story of a scar hanging in the air in the doctor's waiting room. That is when we learn of other doctors who have been unsuccessful in their attempts to modify her scar. In the very last line the man asks the woman's name, something that he thinks will provide information, when in fact it is beside the point next to the story he has just been given. It is merely something for him to possess. When Audre Lorde says she gives us a "new spelling of my name," she insists that the names mean less than presumed, that you have to listen to a person tell his or her own story before assuming what the story holds. Lorde tells her own "story of a scar" in *Zami* and *The Cancer Journals* because she understands the imperative to both gather her multiple selves into one body and to name that body, rather than leave the (mis)naming to another.

Lorde continually states that she claims the different parts of herself—"I am lesbian, mother, warrior, . . ." speaking through difference. It is her credo, a way of living, that all people, but particularly those said to be marginalized, must refuse to be divisible and schizophrenic. It is in the way that she takes us through the history of her body, in both *Zami* and *The Cancer Journals,* that Lorde maps the new terrain of what over one hundred years ago Linda Brent had to whisper and withhold from her readers: all that a corporeal history embodies. The link between Lorde and Brent is crucial: for both, the issue is control over one's own body and the power to see the voice as a literal functioning *member* of the corpus, an organ that works and must be self-tended.

Sexuality is broad and frequently forbidden discursive terrain for many black women in both writing and other sorts of public lives. When we do write, we write our sexualities into existence against a vast backdrop, a history, of misrepresentation and essentializing and perversion, appropriations of our bodies and stories about our bodies. This precedes our entry into the Euro-American written universe. Lorde claims that terrain for herself, defining what she thinks of as the erotic, inscribing in her books an actual, fleshly black woman's body. The effect is like that seen in African-American visual artist Howardena Pindell's 1988 painting, *Autobiography: AIR/CS560.* After a near fatal car crash in 1979 and lengthy rehabilitation, Pindell suffered memory lapses and manifested her process of recovery and remembering in her work. She "used postcards from friends and collected them in her travels to help jar recollections or explain flashes of images. . . . Her automobile accident produced a need for memory."[14] She also began lying on her canvases to leave an imprint of her body with which to work.[15] In the painting, then, Pindell left an impression of her fragmented and reassembled body as physical evidence both that the body exists and that she can imagistically create it. The narrative history of the body is a way of interpellating difference and claiming wholeness.

In Lorde's work, as in Pindell's, it takes literal invasion for the self to be reconstituted. Why is the self not conceived as an a priori whole? These images literalize what is historically and metaphorically true in African-American women's writing: it is the fissure, the slash of the Middle Passage, the separation from the originary, that which the physical scar shows and alludes to—all that is an intractable part of African-American women's history—that makes possible the integrity of the scar, the integrity of the body's history, and a record of what the scar performs.

(1994)

Black Alive and Looking
Straight at You
The Legacy of June Jordan

I have been thinking for a long time about poetry and politics through the instructive examples of June Jordan, the woman and her work. What is the "job" or the work of a poem, and what are its limitations? Why would a writer speak in the morning in the poems, in the afternoon their body while teaching or doing other activist wok, and in the evening in prose essays? What can each form do that the other cannot? Most specifically, what do we want to protect in poetry if we believe, as I do and as Jordan did, that poetry *is* sacred speech that marks the sacred in our lives?

There are poetry people who think that politics, per se, has no place in poetry. This is silly, and it is amazing how strong a hold this idea has had when it is so empty. For time immemorial, across geographies and peoples, poetry has taken as its subject politics, that is, the affairs of the polis, the community and its people. Some people think of themselves as gatekeepers, defenders of a culture, as though culture is something that can be owned by anyone. Culture is like ambient gas; once it is released, there is no collecting it and bringing it back home. This is a great and magical thing: Culture belongs to the world that occasions it. But we could usefully think about the rich and edifying aspects of form that mark discourses in particular genre. How should a poem attend to the business of its chosen form, the care and style with which the box is made rather than what is put inside the box? Poets do have responsibility to make images that compel, to distill language, to write with model precision and specificity that is what poetry has to offer to other genres. It makes something happen with language that takes the breath away or shifts the mind. For the poem, which is after all not the newspaper, must move beyond the information it contains while simultaneously imparting the information it contains. Jordan's commitment to poetry was constant, and it is in those words that we find her simultaneous devotion to the largest possible picture—her keen analyses of the world situation—and to the smallest detail—her tending of language.

Jordan outlines many of these ideas in her book *Poetry for the People*, which chronicles that movement at UC Berkeley, where she taught for many years and offers a try-this-at-home handbook for bringing together people across boundaries through the power of poetry in order, quite simply, to make the world a better place through reading, writing, and performing poetry. To be brave and then be braver. To do the work of learning and knowing so that when you speak to the issues of the world you know of what you speak. To travel, either literally or by learning another language and reading what people who think and speak in that language have seen the world. To come together under the umbrella of poetry knowing not only what we fight against but also where the love is that can unite us. "As I think about anyone or any thing," she wrote, "whether history of literature or my father or political organizations or a poem or a film—as I seek to evaluate the potentiality, the life-supportive commitment/possibilities of anyone or anything, the decisive question is, always, where is the love? The energies that flow from hatred, from negative and hateful habits and attitudes, do not promise something good, something I could choose to cherish, to honor with my own life. It is always the love, whether we look to the spirit of Fannie Lou Hamer, or to the spirit of Aghostino Neto, it is always the love that will carry action into positive new places, that will carry your own nights and days beyond demoralization and away from suicide" (269).

June Jordan lived from 1936 to 2002 and was a poet, activist, essayist, and teacher. She published more critical prose than any other African-American woman writer in the twentieth century, as well as plays, anthologies, children's books, and the tough-minded memoir *Soldier*. She was a proud African-American Brooklynite of Jamaican parentage, but she was not mired in racial, national, cultural, or ideological group-think. She wrote, for example, that after she was raped by a black man "[i]t became clear to me that I had a whole lot of profound and overdue thinking to begin on the subject of what it means to be female regardless of color" (80).

Jordan tirelessly advocated for the rights of others both locally and internationally, and her essays articulated far-reaching, integrated points of view on culture and politics. She is perhaps best known as a prolific poet whose lyrical voice linked political struggle with an ethic of love. Anyone who ever met her knew she was a fierce, brilliant, tireless, brave, direct, luminous woman who exemplified life force even as—especially as—she fought for many years against cancer.

I first read her poems as a child in the beautiful collection *Who Looks at Me* that introduced African-American art to young people. "I am black alive and looking straight at you," she wrote, which always seemed to me to be a credo for moving through this life and its challenges. Her work, then, has always been with me, as has her example of a committed, productive artist, who was sometimes afraid but was always courageous, who saw herself as a citizen of the world, who traveled to Nicaragua and Lebanon and concluded, "The whole world will become a home to all of us, or none of us can hope to live on it, peacefully" (117). She was simultaneously a pacifist and a fighter who knew that "all war leads to death and all love leads you away from death" (121). She wrote, in her unsparing memoir *Soldier,* of the Jamaican immigrant father, Granville Ivanhoe Jordan, who brutalized her, his only child, and yet made her a fighter. That fighter is everywhere in her work: the fighter who, as a student at the University of Chicago, knew that the teacher who told her she couldn't write, who wondered if English was even her first language, was wrong, and would prove him wrong; the fighter who, as a teacher years later, told her students, "this is not my class, this is our class. I do not want to hear what I think. I need to know what you think" (282).

I saw her read several times over the years and was too shy to go up and speak to her. I read every flinty word she wrote—on Chilean poetry, the Palestinian situation, bisexuality, any number of issues of justice—and she became an example to me of someone who made a righteous and beautiful life by poems, essays, and deeds and who did not shy away from what was difficult. A few years ago, when I was about to give a reading in her home of Berkeley, California, I wrote to her, introduced myself, and asked if I could visit her. She responded by giving me a long and magical evening that I will never forget, and an email friendship ensued until she died, just a short year after. There are some deaths where you feel the earth open up and leave a physically palpable void, and June Jordan's death hit me and many others who knew her well and not at all. Her vitality, in word and in person, was extraordinary. Clichés such as "larger than life" and "force of nature" applied. She was utterly beautiful to behold, exquisite and exact and light-filled with an enormous, knowing laugh. She felt like life itself.

In her essay collection *Civil Wars* she wrote of her year teaching at Yale University in 1974–75, where I now teach: her love for students; the particular challenges of teaching "black studies" in the 1970s to "the descendants of slaves as well as the descendants of the slave owners"; and of challenging what she saw as hegemonic worship of Richard Wright in African-American Studies to the exclusion of necessary voices like Hurston's. She decried an "either/or" approach to African-American canon formation and political thinking. "It is tragic and ridiculous to choose between Malcolm and Dr. King," she wrote. "[E]ach of them hurled himself against a quite different aspect of our predicament, and both of them, literally, gave their lives to our ongoing struggle."

At whichever institution employed her she pressed at the boundaries of the place and challenged the status quo. While at Yale she protested an impending campus visit by pseudo-scientific racist William Shockley, and along with students, she organized the Yale Attica Defense. At the anti-Shockley rally, she spoke questions that still echo for us as a community at Yale: "What freedom does this institution care about? Is it the freedom to maintain traditions based on hundreds of years of genocide, theft, rape, humiliation and hypocrisy? Is it the freedom to protect respectability for the forces of conservatism: social, political, academic conservatism: the conservation of bloody, terrifying, life-denying, arrogant traditions of a self-appointed elite of the world? . . . Show me the freedom that this University up-holds: show it to me in its admissions policies. Show it to me in its financial aid programs. Show it to me in its curriculum, in its required readings, in the color, the sex, the viewpoints of its faculty. Show me this freedom that this institutions holds dear." She offered an example for learning, living, and questioning in larger institutional contexts.

And she always wrote about love, be it in a whole book of love poems, *Haruko,* or her constantly asking, Where is the love? Do you know what you are fighting for as well as what you are fighting against? She wrote, "I am saying that the ultimate connection cannot be the enemy. The ultimate connection must be the need that we find between us. It is not only who you are, in other words, but what we can do for each other that will determine the connection" (219). It was love, in her unsentimental vision, that could blaze a path through a world in which multiple-scale violence is the rule.

Jordan wrote, "We need everybody and all that we are. We need to know and make known the complete, constantly unfolding, complicated heritage that is our black experience. We should absolutely resist the superstar, one at a time mentality that threatens the varied and resilient, flexible wealth of our Black future" (284). That "we" is the site of Jordan's poetry, over and over again, real we's of the individuals and communities she has worked with, and imagined we's of the difficult but optimistic future that calls for our clear-eyed love and bravery.

(2003)

Memory, Community, Voice

1. Preamble

At the center of thinking about the cultural production of a group under siege, we must also consider the impediments to our speaking within structures of power that can be soul-crushing. I originally called this essay "Black Poetry in the Age of AIDS." But what is that, precisely? The poetry of black gay men today, which is so ironically coming into collective voice and visibility concurrent with the community's annihilation? The poetry of black women with AIDS, which is little-published and almost impossible to locate? The poetry that any of us might write as we all live in this age? Robert Vasquez-Pacheco writes:

> I've outlasted my lovers, my friends, some of my exes, my tricks, my relatives, even some of the queens I couldn't stand. The guilt of still being alive and healthy. It's funny, there is no satisfaction in that word: outlasted. There is no satisfaction in living longer than friends and loved ones. No catharsis crying at yet another memorial service. I don't go to them anymore. The miracle of survival. Survival is a spot between the rock of guilt and the hard place of memory. . . . History is written by survivors.[1]

Poetic terrain in the age of AIDS includes love, grief, rage, sex, defeat, triumph, despair, death, community, isolation, memory—in short, anything else a great body of poetry might address, and much more than "just" elegy, though students of elegy know that the form at its best is broad and capacious.

The theme of how to remember and how to memorialize our own lives and lives of our more broadly written communities is common both to a consideration of my life as a black feminist and a writer in academia as well as to black poetry in the age of AIDS. So please let this mostly autobiographical meditation be an open door to participate in this thinking about silence and voice, community and context.

2. Amnesia

When my brother and I were small, we used to "play" amnesia. "What's your name?" one or the other of us would say, and the reply would be, "I don't remember." "Where do you live? Who are your parents?" and again, "I don't remember." We thought this was incredibly funny, because, after all, how in the world could you not know who you were or where you came from? I think we had seen too many soap operas where heroes and heroines got knocked on the head and forgot everything, leaving them to either reinvent themselves or be coaxed back to familiarity by anxious loved ones. That was how we ended the game: the memoried one would tutor the amnesiac back by saying, "You live at 819 'C' Street, Southeast, and I am your brother, Mark."

I loved being the amnesiac. I loved the idea that you could make yourself up, or that someone would love you enough to tell you the story of your young life because they wanted you back that much. It was that compulsion to narrativize my individual history and its collective context that compelled me. But now I am faced with a different sort of amnesia. I forget things I think I should remember, such as my entire freshman year in college, when I was profoundly overwhelmed by my first time away from home in an environment that was hostile and nurturing, tedious and thrilling, at the same time. I find that as I gather my thoughts to think about "how I became a feminist in academia," I am "forgetting" many of the stories that might best tell the tale. I think this is because so many of those stories involve the trauma of feeling erased or insignificant in an academic environment, that even my most nurturing of teachers have not been able to make me fully feel that I belong in this kingdom where the life of the mind is guarded. I will never be able to explain to many of my white colleagues the depth of those feelings, nor do I want to.

Numb and no-place is sometimes a tempting reprieve from the hyper-embodied state I am usually in now as a black woman on an overwhelmingly white and male campus, the University of Chicago. It is as though being no-place and having no history could provide a haven from a visibility that feels like all I am, in my classroom, in faculty meeting, and in any number of other campus venues. I don't long for invisibility but rather for the prerogative of going about my business without leaving neon footprints, without having to live so loudly in the categories of "BLACK" and "FEMALE." This hyper-embodied state is made all the more ironic by the fact that my school, with its fistful of black faculty and students, like so many other elite institutions, is in the middle of miles and miles of black people, the South Side of Chicago. The challenge is to find ways to remember without being sucked back into the power deficit that comes with unknowing.

If there is any single thing I have learned from coming of age and being educated in the age of women's studies, it is the importance of remembering, retelling, offering our own narratives that so frequently run counter to official versions of reality. I learned that in college from the writings of Adrienne Rich, Alice Walker, and June Jordan, from the crucial anthologies that gave me so many tools to go forward such as *This Bridge Called My Back, But Some of Us Are Brave,* and *Homegirls.* But remembrance is potent; once its force is unleashed and the status quo named fetid and stagnant, the rememberer is implicitly charged to move forward in that bright light that says, responsibility is yours now. Move. That, I think, is also part of why I can't remember: I don't like remembering all the things I wish I'd said or done differently. I am haunted by my failures to be superwoman who takes on all sexist and racist comers, who sniffs out injustice in its clever guises, who has the power to make bad things stop. If I could break fully through the amnesia, I would be able to answer the question: what happened to the little girl me, who read all the time, who loved to read more than anything except talk, who went to college and took English classes and didn't open her mouth for years?

3. Absence

The first thing to say about "black poetry in the age of AIDS" is that we will not have an opportunity to read it. That is because the people who would write it are dead and dying. That is, more specifically, a statement about the state of writing by black gay men today, who are so vastly affected by the epidemic and who have an identifiable creative community, unlike the many black women with AIDS. Three important anthologies, Joe Beam's 1985 *In the Life,* Essex Hemphill's 1991 *Brother to Brother,* and the black gay collective Other Countries' 1993 *Sojourner: Black Gay Voices in the Age of AIDS,* tell the bluntest truth of the progress of the disease through the black gay creative community; the contributor's notes list more and more who have died or who identify themselves as "living with AIDS" or "seropositive." Hemphill finished *Brother to Brother* for Beam, who died during the course of the volume's production. So many of these writers who would have gone on to leave collections of their own poetry in libraries will simply not live to do that work. Many others are too sick to work steadily; others still write of the struggles to write, to get out any words at all amidst the depression of both their own illness and the decimation of their community.

But Marlon Riggs has also written of how "AIDS can have a liberating effect on the tongue." He continues:

> [S]lowly, gradually, I began to see the consequences of silence, and as a consequence of this insight, my tongue unhinged from the roof of my mouth, dislodged from the back of my throat, slipped—free?[2]

"Slipped" is followed by a dash and "free" by a question mark, the pause and the question inscribing the complicated irony of the writer's self-awareness in the face of a life-threatening disease. That passage speaks a powerful truth about the destructiveness of "silence," which also stands in for living passively in a world that demeans the poor, gay, black, sick, female, where speaking is both self-defense and self-affirmation. But the dash and the question mark—"free?"—mark space for uncertainty about the legacy of "merely" speaking one's truth as one faces fundamental, life-and-death challenges.

Perhaps the most interesting discovery I made in my research is that time and again poetry as a form fails writers trying to write about AIDS. Melvin Dixon is an exception to this generalization. The prose about AIDS is not "better" but is, to generalize, more compelling, as though the compression of poetic form cannot contain the enormity of what the writers are facing. Some of the most memorable work by black gay men, to me, is taking place in performance: Rigg's *Tongues Untied*, Bill T. Jones's dances, Assoto Saint's performance poetry, Pomo Afro Homo's *Fierce Love*. Ironically enough, Riggs works with poetry, but his staging and filming it makes it bigger, louder, wider than the same poems might have been on the page. And so much of this performed work is insistent: insistently refusing to let go of sex, insisting, despite the myriad voices sounding, on collectivity, community, memory.

4. Books

I was born in 1962 and grew up in Washington, D.C. I was, as the author's biographies tend to say, "a voracious reader." My best girlfriends growing up were also prodigious readers. We read together, we talked about books, we acted out scenes from our favorites and we wrote "books" of our own. Our mothers were also big readers. Kerry's mother led our advanced reading group in the library at our school (and was the first to admonish me never, ever, to turn the corners down on book pages); Sarah's mother, a New York sophisticate and herself the daughter of a (female) book editor, filled their home with every book imaginable, and my own mother, as I was proud of proclaiming, read (and still reads) "a book a night." Each of these women, and, consequently, each of their daughters, had a vast array of tastes, so reading could mean *Black Hearts at Battersea, Little Women, The Harrad Experiment* ("What's happening at Harrad?" the cover asked, and I of course wanted to know), the Narnia Chronicles, liner notes to *Jesus Christ Superstar, Whistle for Willie,* Nancy Drew, Laura Ingalls Wilder's *Little House* books, *Our Bodies, Our Selves,* and on goes the delicious list. I learned to read with phonics, red-lettered cards with syllables, the limbs of words, put together with my mother on the rug. Mastering phonics meant that you could read anything at all, even if you didn't understand it. So whether or not we were ready for the books we read, we sucked them all in, anyway.

Those two grainy facts I slipped in a moment ago, "1962" and "Washington D.C.," are relevant in two ways. First of all, we grew up in the age of the women's movement and the civil rights movement. There was a sense of action in the air in the very demonstrations we drove through to get to school and in the work some of our parents, mine included, were doing. We took certain things for granted as far as rhetoric of gender was concerned. "Ms." was immediately adopted in my home when it became common currency (well before the *New York Times* decided it was suitable for adoption) though I would like to make a brief plea here for the uses of "Miss" in African-American culture, where on some blocks there is no greater honor than to be called "Miss Elizabeth" by the children, and an honor of a different order to be called "Miss Thing" [or Miss Anything at all, depending on the circumstance] by black gay friends who wrote the book on diva-dom and its myriad permutations. My grandmother called me "Miss" or "Missy" when I would get too big for my britches, as in, "Well, Miss, we seem to think we're something special, now, don't we?" which of course meant get back in place, curb yourself, don't try to out-diva Diva Number One. Coming out of this context, then, it flabbergasts me to argue today with students who don't understand why it makes a difference if twenty-five year old females are called women or girls.

5. Black

I cannot think about "feminist" without thinking about "black." My developing sense of consciousness was absolutely part and parcel with the formal study of African-American literature and culture. There was no black bookstore in my neighborhood that might have served the function of the feminist bookstore, but I remember hunting through my parents' books for black books, finding Lucille Clifton and LeRoi Jones. Learning about black women came at the same time as my more general education about black people. My important teachers were black and white men, given the demographics of my schools, but my comrades, my greatest teachers, were mostly my black women peers. We shared books and stories with each other, made grand plans to conquer the university, got thrown out of restaurants for talking too loudly, and as Shange writes, loved each other fiercely.

I use the word *black* for many reasons. It is what I was raised on, and old (and, frankly, beloved) habits die hard. Like Gwendolyn Brooks, I like how "black" connects to other black people on the planet, though my context here is North American. And I like how the word glitters with an obsidian power that gets at, again, this interior space I am talking about. "I am black," writes Audre Lorde, "because I come from the earth's inside. Now take my word for jewel in the open light." Black power, black magic, black beauty, black love: how, I wonder constructively, might this exploration of who we are to each other, and how we have struggled with difference, get us to a contemporary usage of those words beyond nostalgia and neo-romanticism? In Kerry James Marshall's paintings, his figures are black-black, a black that is deep, potent, and alive in its density. He writes about his struggle to get the color right, "to [have] that blackness breathe . . . Extreme blackness plus grace equals power." Marshall's black figures become, then, full of light and *visible,* iconic and resonant, a new black they goes beyond both stereotype and romance to poetics.

6. "I think I am smarter than Liz Alexander"

A poetry student of mine, a woman who wants to teach women's literature and who I am relatively sure would call herself a feminist, is frustrated by the way I am teaching her. She has asked me if she has "talent" and I have resisted, explaining that I do not wish to invest myself with the magic-wand authority that bestows talent upon credulous students, that while I am excited by her work and its promise, I am trying to teach her to work for herself rather than for an endowment that I can't really give her, anyway. Dorothy learns in *The Wizard of Oz* that the ability to go home has always been within her, not extrinsic, and all she needs to do is click her heels and she will be there, but the journey has been crucial. However corny, I want my student to understand this, to understand the bind of mentorship, that I can be encouraging without bestowing something upon her and that my working with her in this way demonstrates my faith in her and her writing. I believe this and still do. I want my students to have something that keeps them going from within when no teachers are around saying "yes."

I know that she is angry with me. One day we are having a group conversation about the accouterments of writing—pens and paper and notebook and the like—and she offers her own beautifully covered journal for me to see. "Please, look," she says, and I riffle through the heavy, creamy paper. My eye catches the line, in her handwriting, "I think I am smarter than Liz Alexander." I shut the book quickly and give it back to her.

Now, first of all, "Liz"? Anyone who knows me knows that the diminutive of my name is simply not who I am. Or maybe it wasn't me at all. Maybe there is a Liz Alexander who sits next to her in chemistry. Maybe . . .

But probably not. At a university where I am the only black woman who teaches undergraduates, I cannot help but wonder if this challenge to my "authority" should not be read as necessary hubris from a young woman striving to find her place but rather a much more profound inculcation of the ethos of a university that, at very least by its hiring practices but also by its curriculum, has as much as said, black women are not authorized here.

When I teach black women's autobiography, I find that many of my white women students are at first swept into the class and their experience of me as a teacher by a general sense of sisterhood. But when they listen to some of the hard challenges, explicit and not, that the works make to them as white women, they turn their prickliness on me, challenging my authority. I believe they are responding to feeling displaced in a room where the first-person voices of black women are primary and occupy the "woman" space that some of their feminist education has unfortunately taught them, however implicitly, is the rightful place of white women.

I want to inject them with a serum that makes them believe what I know: that speaking is crucial, that you have to tell your own story simultaneously as you hear and respond to the stories of others, that education is not something you passively consume. And I want, just for a sustained moment, the kind of unarticulated, enveloping mist that shrouds my male colleagues: Respect that does not have to be earned over and over and over again.

7. On Mentorship

And what of my current resistance to mentorship? My mentors, in school, have been mostly powerful black men who thought me clever and worthy of their time and attention. But the soul nurturance has come from women, many of whom were my peers and not my teachers, because the institutions with which I have been affiliated have been largely inhospitable to the presence of black women. White women have been tolerated by these schools to a somewhat greater degree, but I have been sometimes wary that my relations with them might fall prey to the same kinds of knotty difficulties that have affected some of my friendships with white women, no matter how close. More than anything, though, my higher educational experience has been one of disappointment and disillusionment in those who I hoped would be my mentors, and the foolish feeling, at the end of all of this, that maybe I had chosen them badly.

I wish I had earlier understood the pitfalls of being a glittering girl, the smartest girl in the world for a male mentor. Because so frequently that relationship is predicated on a performance by the girl, a performance of her smartness that shows her off as the daughterly possession of her mentor. She makes him look like a good teacher. Her accomplishments make him look like a good feminist. But what happens when she grows, as she must, too big for her britches? When she goes through her Bloomian anxiety of influence, and fights the male mentor to speak her mind? I have seen over and over again strong and brilliant women attracted to male mentors for the power that is usually only theirs to give, falling into a father-daughter paradigm in which their intelligence smiles and beams sunlight onto the mentor rather than existing for its own, glorious, powerful sake.

8. Authority

I thrilled to the Wife of Bath's pronouncement, "Experience, though noon auctoritee / Were in this world, were right ynough to me / To speke of wo that is in mariage." I understood it to mean that her experience in the world of marriage was all she needed to speak with authority of what she knew within that institution, all she needed to authorize herself. But I didn't see that the first go-round. My freshman English teacher was hostile to my baby feminist friends and me, eighteen years old and freshly-minted "Ms." generation high school graduates who came raring to conquer Yale University, when we attempted to press our "feminist readings" on the so-called major English poets from Chaucer to Eliot. This same teacher later became a feminist of some note, but I, for one, never forgave her for not being able to hear us and in some way support our earnest and industrious attempts to read with deep and fresh insight.

I took another class in college on Power and Gender in Renaissance Literature, where the women in the class were silent, the men spoke freely, and the teacher, who was a woman, sanctioned that dynamic by failing to intervene in it. She could have used the very literature we were reading! It is only now, as a professor early in my own career, that I have been able to think back on that, about what it is women students want from us. I have been in public discussions where my own paralysis has made me quiet or less articulate than I can be and kept me, perhaps, from being the role model a young woman needed at that moment. I now choose my battles and deal with the same beleagueredness that perhaps my teachers those years ago felt. I have learned that you can't always be who others need you to be at any moment.

9. What My Grandmother Would Say about the "PC Wars"

Enough is enough. It seems that every day I read something about students' brains softening by the second in women's studies and

various hyphenated-studies classes, and how white n
longer free to speak their minds on campuses, and h
sors are indoctrinating their students into the unholy
race-class-gender, and on and on and on. I think these pu
arguments are designed to keep the progressive-minded
mics who attempted to bring these changes to the acac
busily gnashing their teeth and writing responses to these tirades
while the real work, their work, *our* work, goes undone. I don't
mean to dismiss the very real power of the people who are mak-
ing these divisive arguments, but my instinct is to respond out of
grandmotherly wisdom. *Some people are just limited,* my grand-
mother would say. *Don't follow their agenda. Go about your business.*

10. Coda

As a teacher, my bottom-line challenge seems to be how to bal-
ance passing along to my students the information I have
amassed over my years of study at the same time that I involve
them and empower them to think on their own. Pedagogical
models based on mutual respect are rare; I wish that my at-
tempts to have students fully participate in their learning would
not be seen, as they sometimes are, as free-wheeling, sloppy, an-
archic, out of control: in short, all the awful stereotypes of
women's and ethnic studies.

The first black women received the Ph.D. in 1923, which was
only sixty years ago, and today I am still the only black woman
teaching undergraduates at the University of Chicago, and
many of my other peers are in the same position, so to the anti-
PC forces who rail that the universities are being taken over, I
simply resort to the statistics.

I am truly weary of tooting the same old horn about inclu-
siveness when I am asked time and again, as I have been since
high school, what to do what to do alas alas to bring more
women, more people of color, into the institution. My reading
of this is now fully paranoid: keep me busy repeating the same
old thing that you should have been able to figure out by now
and eventually my brain will go dull and gray and flabby from
inaction.

But in the end, it's all about a couple of jobs for a couple of people, so the ideological lessons learned in women's studies must be applied far beyond the academy, lived in our day-to-day lives, in the way we conduct the business of our lives, in the way we spend our money and raise our children and make a multitude of decisions every day.

As Ntozake Shange writes, bein' a full-grown colored woman isn't easy. But comrades help, books help, and being in an environment that, at least in its rhetoric, says over and over again that you should be treated as a full-grown person, is certainly a start.

When my students tell me *Zami* is "essentialist" and "dated," when they find the love scenes between two women, those that were so exhilarating to my friends and me when they first came out, to be "cornball lesbiana," I have to chuckle (after strenuously trying to show them why I believe otherwise) and think, well, maybe we have come somewhere when *Zami* can be old hat but bedrock, a book they have already read and moved past.

The things I didn't say: Sometimes I drive home from work and scream out the things that I said that didn't sound smart enough until they go away. It isn't enough just to hire women and black people; some of the dirtiest deeds done against me in the academy have been done by white women and black people, even though they operated within a larger economy. No matter how much I prepare for class, I never feel prepared enough for class. I want my students to love me. I won't tell you the names of the books you think I've read I haven't read. I love to read. I love to write. Writing is the way that I remember.

11. Remember

Melvin Dixon meant so much to so many of us. For me, he was a role model in the academy a man of letters, in his own words to me, who never compromised the multiple creative selves that wrote poetry, criticism, fiction, and translation. He taught me to honor all the pieces of my creativity and to define myself, speak my own name in the academy. He also taught me how to finish my dissertation, in a quirky method of threading blank pages through draft typescript but more importantly, one day at a time, clear and steady.

I don't pretend to claim the part of him that was in the eye of the storm of gay communities and AIDS communities. I do, however, think about the way our black communities—men and women, gay and lesbian and straight, healthy and ill—are both singular and overlapping in much the same ways that our own identities are simultaneously fixed and fluid. I think of Melvin's grand poem "And These Are Just A Few," a litany that begins, "This poem is for the epidemic dead and the living. Remember them? / Your neighbors, your siblings, your daughters and your sons," calls names, and ends, "This poem is for the epidemic living and the dead./Remember them, remember me." I first read that poem a year or so before Melvin died, and the poem's final turn, "remember me," hit me square in the chest with what I already knew about his illness. But that was just another way he helped me to grow up—more, I am certain, than he probably knew—by showing me how great writing can make you face the truth around you and within yourself.

You could take that poem and write your own, calling the names of those you've loved and may have lost, saying who they were to you. For remembering is an active charge Dixon makes to each of his readers and I think we must make to ourselves, doing our work and writing in our institutions, living, as we are, in the age of AIDS.

(1992)

Kitchen Table Blues

Meanwhile in Chicago, Miss X and Miss Q meet across the kitchen table:

Miss X: I don't want to watch the march, because I've had a lot of problems with it but was afraid I'd be overcome with emotion when I saw all those brothers together on TV. In the face of all that power, an after-the-fact critique of the Million Man March is like farting in church.

Miss Q: Well, I'm excited. This is history, and you're just full of sour grapes. Why do you always need to be invited?

Miss X: I don't need to be invited. I don't even need to participate. But I will not be told I'm supposed to "stay home" by Louis Farrakhan and Mr. Bankrupt-the-NAACP-Cleaning-Up-Your-Doggish-Peccadillos Ben Chavis.

Miss Q: The march was much bigger than those men, and you know it. What leader isn't flawed?

Miss X: We keep hearing about Farrakhan's anti-Semitism, and that's important. But what about what he says about *us*? "How many times, sisters, have you said 'no' and meant 'yes'?"—that was what he had to say after Mike Tyson raped Desiree Washington. He also said that God created men "a degree above women." I wish a single one of the people upset about his anti-Semitism would also be upset about the way he sees black women. I wish they'd say more about his homophobia, too.

Miss Q: But look at all these men. Only 5 percent of them said they went because of Farrakhan.

Miss X: OK, then here's the rest of my critique. One, the march seems mostly symbolic and without political teeth, like the '63 march and others in which the government was explicitly petitioned. Two, the focus on atonement suggests that institutional obstruction is not the problem and that all black men have to do is face up to their personal responsibility. And most importantly, three: black gender discourse is so utterly impoverished that excluding us this way is bound to make trouble.

Miss Q: Well, there was Betty Shabazz and Cora Masters Barry—

Miss X: I'd rather there be no women at all up there than just the mothers, wives, and widows of the "true" race leaders. It says these brothers don't want us unless we're at home making bean-pies and vegetarian collard greens for our million black children. If anyone's going to be at home, it needs to be these atoning brothers. You retreat to atone. You don't atone in the street for the TV cameras. What really would have been powerful is if the Marion Barrys and Gus Savages up there on the rostrum atoned explicitly for what they've done to black people and black women in particular.

Miss Q: But look at all those black men hugging and saying "I love you." It's like Marlon Riggs in *Tongues Untied:* "Black men loving black men is *the* revolutionary act."

Miss X: And Marlon Riggs is rustling in the grave, because you know he wouldn't have been asked to speak today.

Miss Q: I'm not being sentimental by respecting the symbolic power of the march.

Miss X: I know you're not. I look at all these black men on TV with their power fists, signing and saying, "We are here, we are here." When I talked to my black male friends who went, they said it was the most extraordinary thing they'd ever witnessed. One said, "White people seem so surprised we assembled as peacefully as we did, but to me the important thing was how we showed each other that peacefulness. I saw kids who were straight-up gangsters on the block being kind and courteous to each other. We were the ones who needed to show each other that." It's beautiful—and I want it to mean something more.

Miss Q: You're always going to your black women events. How is what the men are doing any different?

Miss X: Because when we gather it's not in the name of excluding and of coming back and regaining our rightful place on the throne. When I went to a black women's conference last year and there were two thousand of us assembled, I found it literally difficult to focus my eyes because of the ocular unprecedentedness of what was before me: an overwhelmingly white and male university overrun with beautiful black women. I smiled at all of these black women strangers and they smiled back. I don't know what it meant, but it was like seeing the ocean for the very first time. And it showed me how beaten down we usually feel. Those smiles were oases I wanted to suffuse with symbolic might.

Miss Q: That reminds me of the old Amiri Baraka poem, "Beautiful Black Women . . ."

Miss X: Yes, and the poem's a little more complicated than the title. It concludes in the voice of a black man:

> . . . We need you. We are still
> trapped and weak, but we build
> and grow heavy with our
> knowledge. Women.
> Come to us. Help us get back
> what was always ours.
> Help us, women. Where
> are you, women, where, and
> who, and where, and who,
> and will you help
> us, will you open your bodysouls,
> will you lift me up
> Mother, will you
> let me help you, daughter,
> wife/lover, will you

I want to say to the poem, "We're right here in Chicago, if you're looking." He forgot the words *sister, co-combatant, comrade.* But the poem is open-ended. It closes without punctuation—that "will you" is a question, a command, a plea. Its open-endedness means that we are the ones who must step in and finish it right.

(1995)

III

Talking

A Conversation with Deborah
Keenan and Diane LeBlanc

Diane LeBlanc: *Publisher's Weekly* observes that your poems mix a "personal mode" with "prophetic visionary lyrics." How do you respond to that observation? Do you see yourself in the personal mode? Do you see yourself as prophetic? What does that mean to you?

Elizabeth Alexander: I hardly see myself as prophetic. On the other hand, I think of a quotation from Edward Hirsch that I find very useful, in which he talks about the long line in English poetry. The line that exceeds natural breath is the line of prophecy, the line of the dream space, he says. In the book you refer to *(Antebellum Dream Book),* there is that large middle section of poems that had their genesis in dreams and have that sense of spilling over—spilling over into the surreal, spilling past a certain kind of daylight logic, let's say. I think that's something we're used to receiving in the prophetic mode. If you think of the way that we listen to someone like Whitman, or to other people who practice that long line, that may be where your observation comes from. A lot of my poetry comes from "personal" or autobiographical material. What is the transformation that has to happen in order for those details and that realm of personal to work within a poem? I can't really say that I could anatomize it, but I know that there's a transformation that has to take place.

In the workshop today, I mentioned a quotation I've been taking around with me like a mantra lately, from Sterling Brown, through the poet Michael Harper, who quotes from Brown at the end of his collected poems, *Songlines in Michaeltree.* He quotes Brown as saying, "Every I is a dramatic I," which I really love because of the way it has let me think that regardless of whether or not you're working in an autobiographical or personal mode, if there is a persona in the poem, you have certain charges to make it work dramatically in the poem itself. So, fulfilling those demands in the poem as such puts a nice set of parameters around the question of working with the infinite personal, because it's quite infinite.

Deborah Keenan: So both of these are, on one level, removed from the "I" in a certain way.

EA: Do you mean the day-to-day me "I."?

DK: Yes, that's the question we're getting at. What is the "I"?

EA: Yes, one level removed, or alchemized. Or converted, for the purposes of poems, which after all, have very strict demands, a wide-ranging set of demands. I don't think that poems have only one set of strict demands by way of a certain kind of formalism. But at the same time, for any poem to succeed, whatever its rules, there are strict rules, or else the whole thing falls apart.

DK: I'm curious, having read all your books, and taught them, what you consider now to be the major aesthetic events of your life—a particular art exhibit, a certain book, a work of music. Do you have a sense that there are major epiphanies that have come via the aesthetics that have hit you?

EA: I love that question, and I've never thought to answer it before. You always get asked, "What are the books that are important to you? Who are the writers?" I've been trying to think lately what a truly honest answer would be. I've noticed that writers whom I've brought to campus where I teach really resisted this question because, of course, it's always hard to commit, there's so much, and how do you commit? And, also, how do you think about the politics? Not of representation necessarily, although that could be there, but the politics of what your answer is. How do you say something that's useful to people? How do you say something that seems to have some coherent relationship to your work? And of course, it does change. Do you 'fess up to things that were actually quite aesthetically important to you that you would not want to admit that you read or you listen to now?

Usually, as far as writers who have influenced me, I talk about my work as kind of child of Gwendolyn Books and Walt Whitman. Lately I've been thinking about the Lewis Untermeyer *Modern American Poetry* anthology, which I studied in high school. I read it over and over again, and I particularly loved the imagist poets. I loved H.D.; I loved Amy Lowell. Moving out of imagism, T. S. Eliot was very important to me in that high school period. What I hope I've held onto is the real belief that the powerful, distilled, vital image unto itself is somehow enough.

New York City itself was very important to me aesthetically. I was born there—my parents are New Yorkers. They left when I was young and moved to Washington, but with that sense that many New Yorkers have that they couldn't believe they were in this other place and always thought they were going back. I would visit grandparents, particularly a much-cherished grandmother in New York City who had a great deal of time for me and took me on what seemed to me to be very grown-up adventures. The space that she lived in was magical, her objects were magical, her street was magical, and her grocery store was magical. Everything was on a quite different scale from the life that I lived in Washington, D.C. She also took me to musical theater. I think those big, loud, brassy Broadway anthems actually have something to do with my poems.

DK: I think you're right.

EA: Though I've never copped to it before. She also was someone who had a very compelling interest in and respect for other cultures. She lived near the United Nations and was very pleased about that.

DK: We have an amazing image of her hanging out in the stairway, checking out which cultures were coming down the steps.

EA: She grew up in Washington, D.C., and was obsessed with embassies. Imagine that this was the 19-teens and the 1920s, and what the rest of the world must have seemed like, and how she might have imagined it to be.

Also, I grew up taking ballet. Very seriously and quite regularly. I think that listening to music and trying to learn how to make my body do things with music and trying to be, as our teachers would say, sensitive to the music, have a lot to do with trying to have and utilize an ear in poetry. I find that now with certain aspects of my teaching and my approach to certain aspects of craft and discipline.

DL: We can't talk about your work without talking about historical figures and their influences on you. In *The Venus Hottentot* and *Body of Life,* you write in several voices, and historical figures tell their own stories. You addressed this a bit this afternoon, saying you weren't sure why you were talking about the Venus Hottentot, you didn't really know you wanted to write about being on display or about objectification. But as a personal poem, "The Venus Hottentot" becomes historical and autobiographical, is that what you said?

EA: Well, I was saying that in persona poems, sometimes by writing about figures that obsess us, or historical figures, that unwittingly we are activating certain kinds of autobiographical insight and knowledge. We can also trick ourselves into writing about things that feel too close, or too personal, or too undigested, if we were to use the particulars of our own lives.

DL: In *Antebellum Dream Book,* though, you do use more of the personal, of the "I." It seems more autobiographical. Perhaps going back to your earlier response, that it's the dramatic. Can you talk to us about that shift?

EA: Some of it is about getting older. I wrote the first book when I was in my mid to late twenties. I was in school when I wrote the book, so still very much in apprentice mode. In the middle book I was done with school, in very professional years, and then the last book was written after becoming a mother. A lot of women talk about their voices opening up, freeing up, moving toward a certain kind of embracing of their "I." I think that is a rather typical journey you could chart for me.

Also, the particular apprenticeship that I was in and coming out of in the first book . . . I only ever had one poetry teacher, Derek Walcott, who was a great teacher for me. He was, as you would imagine from his work, a strict formalist. He would always say never try to charm in your poems, never try to charm with your identity, it's not enough that you're a cute, black girl.

That was very useful advice, though I was already averse to exploiting "identity." I think the point is, he's saying, none of us as persona is ever enough. Whatever your identity, your set of particulars, there is going to be someone out there who thinks it's fascinating unto itself. But that unto itself doesn't make for a fine poem you could stand up with. So he was also saying, don't be swayed and don't let praise go to your head. And don't let it get into your writing, and don't let it get into your quest. At least, that's how I interpreted it.

Subsequently, you'll see, there is a stricter adherence to certain kinds of forms in *The Venus Hottentot,* and the "I" is a bit under wraps.

DK: It feels that way in *The Venus Hottentot.* I didn't ever think of the "I" as under wraps; I think of the word *guarded*. It ends up getting attached to that lyric "I" sometimes, in the first book. Whereas in the third book, the "I" feels like a shield has been thrown up to the sky. It's interesting, these three journeys are so different.

In Rafael Campo's poetry, there's a lot of "what the body told," and he often finds his energy as poet in what the body told. It always feels to me that the material world, whether it's in paintings or your body, is an incredible anchor to you. Even though we think you're getting unfettered—like we were reading "Creole Cat" the other night, you know, you took those three steps and you fly. But you were instantly back, anchored, grounded in your body again.

I think you've been really faithful to what the body told. What do you feel you've stayed faithful or connected to? Has your faith stayed steady to a certain set of allegiances as a writer? Or do you feel like you've tossed them over your shoulder?

EA: I've developed a great deal more faith in whatever the truly inner voice is. I've kept sporadic journals for a long time. Every now and then, when I look back at them, even going back into my teenage years, I'm struck at how I have some of these very strange little utterances, clusters, things that were frightening to me when I wrote them, that felt unrecognizable to me as the self that I spent most of my time walking around in, but yet, I wrote them down. I had to write them down. The ongoing quest is to trust the voices that are more and more and more subterranean. And to trust, also, the sense of shape that arises from those voices.

I think that my second book—this is really putting it in too much of a nutshell—but in some ways I think of it formally as a transition. You know, what happens if I open up this line? Because there are a few very-long-line poems in the second book, and those were big moments for me, to write those poems: "In the Small Rooms" and "Haircut." Those were breakout moments, and the title poem was, too, but it was also terrifying. I didn't know if I had hit something that was cohesive.

I just saw Richard Wilbur on a panel discussing what form is for him. He said, "If I start a poem and finish half of it and go to sleep and then wake in the middle of the night wanting to finish, if I don't know that I'm writing a rondeau, how do I know how to finish it?" That was interesting. In a way, even though the forms I work in now are not only sonnets or villanelles or rondeaus or this, that, and the other thing, I like the idea that there are a whole lot of shapes out there, but that you do always have that sense of shape in your head. Sometimes, it's just a curious and unfamiliar shape, and you have to trust that it's a shape, that the bowl has sides, so I think that's what the sort of developing faith would be all about.

DK: So you're saying, it's keeping a sense of belief in yourself. That the shapes you're coming up with in dream, or walking around, might hold what you need to say.

EA: Yes. And I wouldn't call that being faithful to "myself." I would call that being faithful to some sense of shape or vessel.

. . . .

DK: I have two quotes. Stanley Kunitz said, "Never before in this, or any other country, have so many apprentice writers had the opportunity to study with their predecessors and their ancestors. That is one explanation of why it is so difficult to detect and to find a generational style in the work of our contemporaries. Instead, we have an interfusion, an amalgam of styles and influence, a direct transmission belt that overleaps the age barrier. A two-way learning process culminating in the young writing old, the old writing young."

And Susan Ludvigson, in the fall 2003 issue of *Water-Stone*, talks beautifully about the lessons she's getting from her students. Her young students say, "Read this, read this." It's blasted her whole vision of her line into a whole new world, in that spirit.

So here's what I'm wondering: What direct transmission do you think you've received from your elders? I know you've mentioned a few of them, but beyond the ones you've mentioned.

And, are there younger writers who are coming on, and you're going "oh" and then you go home and think, "wow." Then, do you have a sense in any of your books that you would say, "I speak for my generation"?

EA: For the last six years, I've taught at a workshop called the Cave Canem Poetry Workshop for African-American writers. Toi Dericotte and Cornelius Eady founded it out of their own experience, which is like so many of our own experiences—being either the only one teaching mostly white students, or having an empathic feeling about the only student of color, or one of just a few. And asking the question, what would happen if we created an environment in which the poem itself, in all that that means, could really be explored? It's been a completely remarkable community. The writers have ranged in age from nineteen to eighty-one. Most people, I would say, are maybe thirty, who are working, who've done undergraduate degrees, but it truly varies. Often this propels them into an M.F.A. program because they get really excited and confident about the work they do and they have a portfolio to present.

There are a lot of writers in that group who are fierce. I'm thinking of one in particular, Terrance Hayes, whose second book, *Hip Logic,* just came out from the National Poetry Series. I've taught his work. His first book was much more discernibly an "I" that was presumably close to his life—a young, black man who had a difficult relationship with his father. These are some of the sociological particulars of the book, that he said have led a lot of people to feel that that is the more accessible book, that's the book they think is the better book because it's telling the story they want to know, or the story they know how to receive, about a young, black man. In his second book he has a lot of surreal dips, really surprisingly surreal dips, and it is exciting to see him trust in that way. He also has some acrostic word game poems, where he starts off with a word game in a newspaper and then he makes quite remarkable poems out of them. But these are harder for some people to receive, in part because they confound the stereotypical expectation of who the young, black male poet should be, and what his aesthetics should look like.

Bob Kaufman is a poet who's been very important to Hayes, and it's also important to him that Kaufman has not received that kind of attention that Baraka, or other sorts of poets who are his peers have. So Terrance is a young writer I can think of whose work makes me so excited and proud and challenged, and just the ongoing life that comes out of that group, and joy for writing poetry, are sustaining and inspiring. I don't ever lose that joy, but you know, I get a little tired sometimes. And to feel that every summer that I've gone there, I teach and I read, I feel like I have to come up with some hot new stuff. I get very nervous about sharing for this group that is, in many ways, one of my ideal audiences: people who just are very serious, committed people who know where I'm coming from. You don't often know who your audience is, of course, because the poems go flying out into the air.

And then elders, I would also say Robert Hayden. I mentioned his name, but he's been—his exquisiteness, his—he called himself a romantic realist, which I like quite a bit, a believer in beauty, a believer in universality in the truest, most rich kind of sense, but also very wedded to the particulars of Paradise Valley, the Detroit neighborhood that he writes about, or any place where he is. The ways that he has, in a poem like "Frederick Douglass," wonderfully acknowledged what heroes mean to us, but also undercut, you know, that hero to us, not with statues, rhetoric, and bronze alone. . . .

Lucille Clifton's work was very important to me when I was younger, and still is. She's an amazing poet. I call her the "Still waters run deep poet," because as a younger person I thought that I could understand what the poems were saying. But they get under your skin, and they reveal themselves and their depth and nuance and lessons over time in such a remarkable way. My parents had lots of books, but not many poetry books, but when I was young they had Lucille Clifton's *Good Times* in the house, and so I read it over and over again.

DL: I want to talk a bit more about Robert Hayden, in the context of your essay "Meditations on 'Mecca': Gwendolyn Brooks and the Responsibilities of the Black Poet." You write that in addition to being faced with racism, black writers face judgment within their communities. You explain the pressure to create work that will "perform a certain service as well as say and not say what is empowering or embarrassing to the race at large." I think of your poem "Race" in *Antebellum Dream Book* as a good example. In your essay, you quote Robert Hayden saying that he identified himself first as a poet and then as a black. He later revised that to say poets' work should be universal, so it should be addressing issues of race and other large issues if it's compelling, urgent work. Now, I recently read your essay from 1994, "Memory, Community, Voice," and you say, "I cannot think about feminist without thinking about black." So, to put these all together, I'm wondering what you consider your responsibilities as a black, feminist writer today?

DK: We really want you to speak to this whole idea of how many words drop in front of the word *poet,* and does that empower, does it limit?

EA: I've thought a lot about this, over a long period of time. Once, with some of the Cave Canem poets, we made up a great game, where you had to fill in the blanks, "I come from a long line of . . ." Then we did, "I come from a short line of . . ." My answers surprised me. I come from a long line of "race people," I said, people whose work has been about bettering the race in one way or another. Their sense of themselves in the world has been about bringing black people along with them.

At the same time, there are so many different ways that I have seen that sense of responsibility enacted. It can be in your job, or it can be in the way that you are in your neighborhood, or it can be the way you teach your children. In the case of this grandmother that I mentioned, in the proud way that she dressed and appeared and conducted herself, she was really quite fabulous, and quite composed, and quite impeccable and conscious, and she believed that she was quietly slashing down dragons along the way. So there are a lot of different ways that people interpret this whole business of race responsibility.

When Hayden was talking about being a poet first, I interpreted what he really was saying was that if you are doing the job of writing a poem, that is the job you're doing. I mean really, the difficulty is with the question. I understand why people ask that question, "Are you with us or are you not with us? How do we move forward?" But it's not a good question; people don't often segment themselves so starkly. Even though I'm sure I've asked versions of that question. Are you in, or are you out?

I think that was Hayden's insistence, saying I'm a poet first. The fact that I attend to the poem doesn't take away from anything else, doesn't take away from writing *Middle Passage* in 1946. Before half the people who criticized him had even written a word. You know, it doesn't interfere with that, and that's what I take from the lesson of Hayden.

So that in that essay that you quote from, and looking at Hayden around '68, '69, '70 and looking at Brooks around '68, '69, '70, Brooks is now supposed to be the black woman poet, because she's had her conversion, and she's with the people, and Hayden is the Uncle Tom. But at the same time, in the books they wrote at that time, both included Malcolm X poems; both included poems about black heroes, the same topics from a different angle. Brooks and Hayden faced the same challenges as different human beings, but as committed human beings, and as committed, black human beings.

I try to remember that you can get really distracted by the demands people make on you. Demands that are real are one thing, demands that come from a real community in need, or a real person in need. We're asked all the time to be of service. But demands that are about posturing—you may have to deal with them, but I'm trying to figure out a way not to let them worm their way in too much.

I was giving a talk about a week ago at Southern Connecticut Community College, which is about two miles away from Yale, where I teach. There are all kinds of issues with how Yale functions within the New Haven community, so forth and so on. One of the faculty members said, "So how's it feel breathing the rare, fine air over there at Yale?" I didn't get bent out of shape; he felt had to ask the question. It gave me an opportunity to talk about my students. What do you know about my students and what their backgrounds and struggles are, and how they come to Yale University? What do you know about me as one of a few black woman teachers at a school where there is only one tenured African-American woman in the faculty, and it's not me? And there has only been one tenured African-American faculty member for years and years and years. Our visible work lives are one part of our lives, but I travel and go to different places where I read and teach, and I also teach at Cave Canem,

I have children, I have ten billion nieces and nephews, I have strangers I correspond with. I mean, there are all of these different ways that each of us acts and takes responsibility for "the community." And so, I guess, how do you sleep at night, just with the sense hopefully, that you do your best when you can.

DL: As far as the feminism aspect of that, Barbara Smith says you just can't pull the pieces apart.

EA: I love Barbara Smith, and I don't think you can. I think that's a very important stance to take, when, for example, in anti-discrimination law, if I'm a black woman and something bad happens to me and someone calls me a so-and-so and so-and-so at my job, I have to decide whether I'm going to sue as a black person or as a woman. You know, well, what was the worst part of what was said to me? That will make you crazy.

But we have such a long, inspiring, tough history of African-American women finding ways to maneuver. It wasn't until I think the late 1960s in the American South that a white man was ever convicted of raping a black woman. So, you have a whole legal history that says that what you know never happened. How do you maneuver a way around that? How do you stay sane? How do you survive?

The words of Audre Lorde have been really important to me—that refusal to separate. With so many essays, she writes, I am woman, mother, dyke, black, New Yorker, so-and-so and so-and-so. Don't divide yourself, because other people will try to. Say who you are because no one will name you kindly. I think that's crucial. She gave it to us so clearly. She's on the elder list.

DK: This is the last quote I'm going to read to you, from Vassar Miller. She says, "Poetry, like all art, has a Trinitarian function: creative, redemptive, and sanctifying. Creative because it takes raw materials of fact and feeling and makes them into that which is neither fact nor feeling. Redemptive because it transforms pain, ugliness of life into joy, beauty. Sanctifying because it gives the transitory a relative form of meaning." I love these categories and thought hard about them for a lot of years. Do you feel like you're carrying big, abstract nouns around, that are your set? Like Vassar Miller felt these are her set?

EA: Those are really good. I don't think that way. What I do carry around is that sense that we live in the word. And the word is precious, and the word must be precise, and the word is one of the only ways we have to reach across to each other, and that it has to be tended with that degree of respect. That is the kind of human level of, "If I'm not precise with my word, if I'm not good with my word, then how can I come soul to soul with anyone else?" I do carry that around. And also, the idea of transformation. I believe that life itself is profoundly poetic, in all sorts of places and guises and unexpected places.

Audience Question: Harryette Mullen was here and gave a beautiful reading from her book called *Sleeping with the Dictionary.* One of her comments was about how she's felt that there's been so much pressure on African-American writers to stay in the oral tradition—her first book was praised for being within that tradition—and she wants to create more space for writers to work with whatever form their voices lead them to. I'm just wondering if there's more you'd like to comment on, as far as what the canon is, and pressure you felt to write one way or another.

EA: I'm so glad you mention Harryette Mullen because she's a genius. She's really an extraordinary thinker and prose writer, as well as a poet. Harryette is a writer whom I consider a generational peer, to pick up on the generational aspect, and whom I also think of as being—because she has a real academic career as well—I think of her as being analogous, in a way. That book really makes me want to write because it awakens me to the possibilities of a language. She has such a sense of play—you see that in her mishearings, you know, all of those phrases that she twists just a little bit. It's as though the whole history of the usage of a word and a phrase comes spilling out, and also a future opens up in front of it. So, she's very, very remarkable. And her example challenges me to be a better writer.

Audience Q: Can you talk about your process? How do you write a poem?

EA: The process starts with a word or a phrase, or an image, or sometimes the utterance goes bit past the phrase. Just when you get on a roll, the kinds of things that come, always, it seems while driving the car or doing other things that hopefully you keep track of. I also keep in my notebook, and in my file folder, newspaper clippings, pictures, things that should be saved.

When there is time to sit down and work, there are a lot of

different starting points. But it all begins with utterance, with word, even if then it grows into, as with the Amistad poem, an idea for a poem. Or even with something like the long poems, like the Ali poem. It began with an obsession with him, and a sense of trying to enter him through his language, rather than, I'm going to write a poem. It's going to have twelve parts. It's going to be in the voice of Muhammad Ali.

Audience Q: We read *The Venus Hottentot* in class, and we watched the film and looked at the stories of Venus Hottentot. I was struck by how much there is to the story. How did you distill down what you wanted to talk about when there was such a huge story there?

EA: That poem is very important to me, but I don't remember much about writing it. Which is to say, it wasn't quite written in a white heat, but it was written in a very, very, very consuming space. The first words that came to me were, "I am called Venus Hottentot," and the thought of being called other than the name your mother and father gave you, and living your life that way. Then the challenge was how to hear her voice, and how to hold onto her voice. It seemed very important that the voice be very tight, and very consistent.

I recently read a book by a poet named Peg Boyers called *Hard Bread* that's told from the imagined voice of Natalia Ginsberg. It brings up a lot of questions, too, about when you have an interesting life, a life that contains volumes. How do you decide what you are going to choose, and how do you also not approach it as reportage? Because that's not what your job is, as a poet. Your job is to transform in some way. And yet, that process, I think, is mysterious.

For me, it started with getting a sense of what her voice was, what her rhythm was. And making sure that the other voices were tight and consistent. It also is a poem that has a huge amount of historical research in it. Even though most of those details didn't make their way in in a visible fashion, it was very important to know.

Audience Q: Do you think of white versus black when you write celebratory poems about African-American historical figures? What do you imagine reaching across to that audience? Does that play into your creative process?

EA: It does not play into my creative process, and I think that would be a bad thing. Because to be presumptuous about any kind of audience is not a good thing. I've had too many wonderful surprises. I don't even mean it to say, "Oh a white person loved this black poem." I don't mean that at all. But I've had many surprises with people who read poetry who I wouldn't have imagined read poetry, that it has a place in their lives. You just really never know. You just can't let that imagining get into the creative process because it would twist it and distort it and shut it down. After all, what individual people are we talking about? Some people talk about the ideal reader, and I don't really have an ideal reader. I read the poems out loud to my husband when I write them, and he gives me the thumbs up or thumbs down. *(Laughter.)* But you know, I'm just trying to be my most articulate self. I just trust that when it goes out there, it will be found by who ever can make use of it.

I can't think of a poet who comes from my exact background. I mean, there are African-American poets, but Robert Hayden's life was nothing like mine. Gwendolyn Brooks's life was different from mine. I feel a kinship with the reverence with which she speaks about her parents. I identify with her as a mother, and we share a love of Chicago. But she had a very different life. The beautiful thing about poetry is that you never know who will find it, and you never know what will be found in it.

Audience Q: How do you make time for the work? Your life is very complicated. You teach full-time. You have children and a husband. Your mind is taken up by a lot of thought and critical work. How do you make time for the work?

EA: Before I had a family to tend to, it seemed that there was never enough time either. But in fact, actually, paradoxically, there's more time because now I know the value of it a bit more. What I used to do was think of the summers. Twice I went to a writer's colony, and that was amazing to have those three weeks to go and only have to worry about the writing. To get so much done that I was jump-started. You kind of get the muscles going again and you keep it going a little bit more. So those summer respites were very important. I don't do that anymore. I just try the best I can to keep track of the scraps as they come, and make the time when I can. It tends to happen in jags. And in those jags other things kind of fall by the wayside, you know, bills don't get paid, and things get a little piled up and then I emerge and tighten things up again.

I wasn't able to write prose for several years, right when my children were babies. I found that prose took a space that was just too wide, and I couldn't find it, and it also distracted me for too long. I'm interested in how poets like Lucille Clifton, who had six children, talk about having a room of one's own. She says, "For me, the ideal circumstances for writing a poem are at the kitchen table. The kids have the measles, and everything is going around." What I love about that, and what I think is really useful and important is that idea of being porous. How can you stay porous at the same time that you have your bubble, in which things can exist or stay safe?

(2003)

Who Is the Self in Language? /
Rooted in Language

An Interview with Meta DuEwa Jones

Meta Jones: Your poetry has explored the dynamics of enslaved Africans and resistance through Sartje Baartman, Nat Turner, and others. In "Islands Number Four," you "describe a slave ship in 1789 . . . Up close, bodies / Doubled and doubled, serried and stacked." This is dated before the 1839 Amistad Revolt. In your new book of poems, *American Sublime,* you have an epic poem called "Amistad." Did earlier poems such as these foment your interest in the Amistad affair? Were you also motivated by its close proximity—the ship was brought into New London, Connecticut, and the enslaved Africans were detained in New Haven—to you, personally, geographically, and politically? Why did you choose to explore this historical and political imbroglio?

Elizabeth Alexander: Seven years ago I was walking my first son in the stroller through New Haven. We came upon the New Haven Historical Society and I thought, why have I never been in here? Once inside, we saw the original of the famous portrait of Cinque as well as other documents from what you aptly called the "political imbroglio," and I realized that not only was there much more to know than I did but also it made me think about the ground on which I walked, New Haven, Connecticut, and what I could learn about its history. The story brought in Yale and teaching, which was of course of great interest to me, and I thought that perhaps in poetry I could imagine my way to a fresh understanding of some aspects of the affair.

MJ: Your treatment of the translator, James Covey, for instance, does seem to freshly imagine, or "translate" this affair in ways that one wouldn't find in government documents, historical texts, or film. The search for someone fluent in Mende to enable the jailed Africans to have their say in court must have had great implications for you as a poet.

EA: The character Covey was close to my heart. He himself was brought from what is now called Sierra Leone in the slave trade and became a dock worker in New York. Many years after he was brought to the United States he was found by the Yale professor Josiah Willard Gibbs who was looking for someone who spoke Mende who could help the captives tell their story. What would that moment of being spoken to in your language after so many years feel like? What would it mean to meet with those captives after being away from home so long? What new identity would Covey have had to assume in order to survive? Where does what you leave behind after that violent separation reside?

MJ: What process of selection framed your ordering and titling of *American Sublime*? How important are details such as poem order and arrangement to you in the development of your creative statement?

EA: The title *American Sublime* operates many different ways: it is literal, as in the poem "American Sublime," to describe paintings out of that school and time period, but also ironic, because those paintings were made in the midst of a violent slave economy. In the *ars poetica* poems, part of what I realized is that I have always reveled in the possibilities of American Englishes, its sublimities. So "Sublime" is sometimes literal and sometimes ironic, and "American" is meant to contain all of the possibilities, erasures, and contradictions of American-ness and the American story.

MJ: In "First Afro-American Esperantist," you invoke both the literal and metaphoric possibilities of "lingua franca" as well as the interplay between identity, audience commodity and language. I love the history, music and politics your phrase "dialect bucket" conjures. Could you comment on this poem?

EA: Isn't that a quirky little poem? There actually *is* a first Afro-American Esperantist—William Pickens—and there is a certificate that says so among his papers. He went to Yale in the early twentieth century. There is such beautiful hope in the idea of Esperanto, the wish to communicate across place and boundary, and I think I am also interested in what we might call

Negro esoterica—I love our quirks and oddnesses, our particularities, and my poems are sometimes a way to make an archive, to preserve them.

MJ: You also seem able to make the archive come alive, to give flesh and bone to the historically important figures you write about, from Paul Robeson's wife, Eslanda, to James Vanderzee to Yolande Dubois to Muhammad Ali. Does working with major figures from a previous epoch or era present particular challenges, offer special rewards?

EA: The study of African-American history and culture has been a great gift to my work, because the font of rich stories and characters appears limitless.

MJ: You've mentioned history and culture. Is *spirituality* also a vital component in your work? I do not intend to suggest religiosity, but instead the human and heavenly nature of the spiritual: divination, intuition, the incorporeal. Yet you have simultaneously written a great deal about corporeality. How do you keep these in balance? How does spirit inflect your writing?

EA: Writing poetry seems to be a way that I explore such questions. Spiritual and ethical situations and conundrums are occasions for poems—though I am rarely aware of the conundrum as such when I embark upon the poem—and the writing of the poem is a way of working through those conundrums and accepting their frequent open-endedness. Besides making and raising children, the mystery of making art is the most spiritual zone of my life.

MJ: Yes, *family*, literally—in terms of kinship—and figuratively—in terms of community, appears as a recurrent theme in your work. How has family influenced your creative process, conceptually or concretely, your career as a professional writer?

EA: I'm very lucky in the family department. I come from and have joined with clear, committed people, whatever they do. I think they have affected me most in the way of being a teacher and being someone who always feels I am supposed to be helpful to others and generous. That's the family ethic.

MJ: You have written of Gwendolyn Brooks's "specialized vocabulary . . . the strange diction that could belong to no one else; the tensile strength of each line. Your poetry's specialized vocabulary includes words such as *angostura, damask, finger-fucked, gelatinous, Mende, tonsured, tulle, viscous, Whassup G,* and *ziggurat.* As you observe in "Fugue," "You could / ruminate all night about / the difference between 'taut' / and 'tight.'" Can you comment on the words you use in your work that incite curiosity, surprise, and delight?

EA: That is what writing poetry is for me, on a level, the profound—and I do mean profound—pleasure of writing certain words, preserving them, giving them a place to be and make sense and raise new questions and possibilities.

MJ: Let's turn to a question that your poetry asks and answers in a variety of ways. In your poem "Haircut," the speaker begins by "getting off the IRT in front of the Schomburg Center for Research in Black Culture" in New York and ends by asking, "What is black culture?" How might you answer the question: What is black culture? How does it impact your life, your poetry, your writing in general?

EA: On one level, we need to remember that any culture is that which makes its way to an audience. As critics and scholars and appreciators of art, what we can talk about is what we have received, and much has not made its way to us or has only begun its journey to limited pockets of the populous. Marketplace issues very much affect what we even think of as culture of any kind. That said, black culture is that which black people have made across an unimaginably wide spectrum of backgrounds, aesthetics, and identities. And we have not yet fully taken stock of all that black people have made under the rubric of culture because I think that there has been too much that's getting stuck in prescriptive ideas of blackness. We get caught up in the politics of, is it black enough? Does it follow this particular trajectory?

MJ: Your definition, "Black culture is that which black people have made," reminded me of an interview with Gwendolyn Brooks in which Brooks says, "The black poet should only write about the black experience," which sounds proscriptive but she insists, "The black experience is *any* experience any black person has."

EA: Absolutely. It is really too astonishing in 2005 that the widely defined mainstream imaginary still sees black people in such limited terms. You know the feeling when a white person is looking at you or listening to you speak as though you could not possibly exist?

MJ: Yes. Absolutely.

EA: No matter how devoted we are to the culture and to each other, we have a lot to overcome, imagining ourselves, or imagining each other. And in receiving each other.

MJ: Your recent essay collection, *The Black Interior,* imaginatively covers a range of subjects, including close textual readings of literary works, film, and other dimensions of popular culture. You move from talking about the nineteenth-century black intellectual Anna Julia Cooper to poets such as Langston Hughes and Michael Harper to *Jet* magazine to an extended meditation on Denzel Washington. The book's form and subject make it conducive for an undergraduate Introduction to African-American Studies course. What kind of pedagogical contribution do you envision your work making?

EA: I've been teaching at universities for a long time now, and so certainly some of the ideas in the book have gotten their start in the classroom. I've tried them out in the classrooms, and one of the things that I really love, and one of the reasons that I never have and never want to write exclusively, is that staying engaged with the literary and cultural traditions as a teacher, you have to keep going back to the texts. That's the pleasure of university teaching for me. And so it wouldn't be surprising if that pleasure and that practice made its way to the book.

The essays formally are whatever they have to be. When you talk about Anna Julia Cooper in the nineteenth century, she had to invent a form that served her unimagined "type," that type being the turn-of-the-century African-American female intellectual. So she used the first person. She quoted from scripture. She commented on world literature. She engaged what we would now call political science. She made her way and this made space for her mind, and then she was visible, imaginable, plausible, real. I've always been interested in the kinds of essays that cross genres and follow what I would call poetic logics and stretch the way we think about the essay, and stretch the way we think about thinking and defining arguments in a wider way. I've always written critical prose but I've also always wrestled with how to call upon all of my aesthetics and intelligence at the same time, when it felt that it did not fit into received forms.

MJ: I want to turn to your first book of poems, *The Venus Hottentot.* Your later titling of the collection *The Black Interior* seems apt since your poems address the intersectionality of race, gender, sexuality, class. Particularly the issue of the literal black exterior in terms of Saartjie Baartman's exoticized and exploited exteriority, through the public display of her body in Europe. On the other hand your poem envisions Baartman's willful negotiation and protection of her interior self. As a black creative and critical writer are you continually negotiating the interior and the exterior self in your work?

EA: I often say when I do teach creative writing that it's all well and good to have an idea, to say, I want to write about such-and-such and such-and-such. But I think the idea has to be rooted in language. It has to live in language. You can talk forever about the idea of the Venus Hottentot. But the first line of that poem which came to me, "I am called Venus Hottentot," was a real voice speaking and saying, essentially, I've been called out of my name. The name my parents gave me is no more. I am called Venus Hottentot. That's the language part, where character lives. That is what we have to protect and that is very challenging for black writers because of how challenging it is to be a social creature in the way black people are forced and called to be. Obviously I don't mean social creatures like just hanging out. I'm talking about what it means for us to walk around in the world as physical people and actually deal with stereotypes and expectations that deny our own complex interiority.

This is what I explored in the dream poems of *Antebellum Dream Book.* I imagined I would find a sort of "fictional space" in the dream world, but what I found instead was space that was wild and intimate and raced and gendered. So it's not about kind of superseding the social identity, but it is about protecting the full dimension of the self. Anything and everything that black people are.

MJ: That's lovely. Rooted in language. It's not just this idea—what happened to Baartman—but the poetics of her saying: "I speak English. I speak French. I speak Dutch and languages Cuvier will never know have names." You wrote previously that despite the plethora of visual imagery surrounding The Venus Hottentot, her voice was absent from the historical register. And that poem is in part about giving voice rooted in poetic language. And that is what makes it art.

EA: That's what catches the imagination of somebody else, a listener or reader. Even the way that we express ourselves as non-poet "civilians," if you will, is what makes us interesting to other people. What stops you on the bus when you overhear a conversation is the way people use language. Who is the self in language? And what is the revelatory and unguarded and surprising self in language? That's what makes someone else pay attention. When you start turning that into art, that's what making poems is about.

MJ: Is there, for you, a distinction between making poems and making essays? As the author of what reviewer Donna Seaman called three "indelible" poetry collections, why a book of essays as opposed to another volume of poetry?

EA: I worked on the essays of *The Black Interior* for a long time over time and simultaneous with poems. There is a lot of subject matter that doesn't quite work for poems, or that perhaps can go in both directions. Often I cannot answer. Because again, there's a lot of reading and research and thinking in my poems that is not necessarily made explicit. There are a lot of arguments in my poems. There's a lot of narrative in my poems. Why in a given moment do I turn right or do I turn left? I'm just not sure how that happens. One of the things that I enjoy in essays is—I'm very opinionated, very declarative and I like being able to plainly state certain things or try to convince with textual, often close reading. In a poem I think you just are supposed to be there, and if somebody wants to come be in your world, you being the poem, then they can come there, but poems are not primarily meant to work to convert or charm, though of course they can and do. In essays, as in teaching, I enjoy that work of saying, okay, come on, are you with me? Though I wanted the essays to be completely clear, I wanted them also to do things that were mysterious and evocative and, therefore, interesting over time, too. In a way that poems remain mysteries to me, even if I have written them, even if I—if I lived with them for a very long time.

MJ: You invoked the joy of teaching. You've been involved as

160

a teacher both within the university classroom and in your role as an instructor and mentor to many poets through the Cave Canem organization. Could you describe your involvement in Cave Canem and its significance as a literary and cultural institution?

EA: We really are in the middle of a black poetic renaissance, in different cultural locations. It's all over the country. Many more black poets are getting published than in previous years. They're getting published by black presses, and they're getting published by white presses that never published black people in their lives. Our work varies tremendously, stylistically and thematically. Black poets are in creative writing programs where we never were before. And while that's not totally taking care of some of the isolation and some of the issues that were problems, nonetheless, to sound old for a moment, when I was coming along, the moment was not like this. It was not like this. And so it's really very exciting and remarkable. What Cave Canem most potently represents to me is the incredibly rich and healthy and loving, yet challenging, diversity among ourselves and our aesthetics. Because there is no one aesthetic or doctrine in Cave Canem between the faculty or the fellows. So many of the fellows have published books and are very well known, and have remarkable careers of their own—Major Jackson, Honoree Jeffers, A. Van Jordan, Evie Shockley, Tyehimba Jess, and many others. I am proud that at Cave Canem we have made the commitment to help sustain, challenge, and develop whatever the best of each other is. By taking some important intracommunity historical lessons very seriously, we are also trying not to litmus test each other into extinction.

MJ: When you talk about a black poetic renaissance, it directly links to your earlier discussion of the expansiveness of what one black aesthetic or cultural experience might be or look like. The lineage that Cave Canem has helped to create also connects to the presence of other contemporary literary institutions that have supported writers of color such as the Hurston-Wright Foundation, the Dark Room Collective, the Voices of Our Nation Arts Foundation, and so forth. These enable us to review what has been happening with black poetry and preview its future development.

EA: You don't have to be a scholar to be aware of the fact that ongoing availability of our work is an issue. I've spent a lot of time in the Beinecke Rare Book Library at Yale, especially around the James Weldon Johnson collection. It's very humbling. You see the amazing writing in *Negro Digest* by the people who never went on to publish books, who would only be known through those periodicals. You see letters from important poets late in life practically begging for readings and publication. You see exclusive first editions of poetry that have been out of print for forty-five years. The reality is that most people will never know these books even exist. That's why I keep coming back to the institutional aspects of work being available.

MJ: Emphasizing the institutional aspects is crucial since it counters the idea of the isolated individual artist. Poetry is an individual *and* institutional *and* communal and cultural endeavor.

On another topic, critics and reviewers often use the oral, the vernacular, and the musical as a rubric for interpreting black writers' work. Yet a long history exists of black poets' deep investment in collaborations with visual artists. Langston Hughes and Roy De Caravas would be one well-known example, as might Ishmael Reed's work with Betty Saar in the seventies, or, more recently Alison Saar's collaboration with Erica Hunt, or Kevin Young's work on Basquiat. Your newest volume, *American Sublime,* as you mentioned, evokes that visual impulse, as does your previous writings on James Vanderzee, Romare Bearden, as well as the impressive array of book cover art in your collections. Can you talk about your choice of book cover art?

EA: I'm so proud of my gorgeous book covers, all of which have important works by African-American artists on the cover: Charles Alston, Kerry James Marshall, Carrie Mae Weems, Bob Thompson, Elizabeth Catlett, Henry Ossawa Tanner, and Betye Saar—so far! I think it is an opportunity not only to expose my readers to that great work but also to make an implicit conversation between the poems and the paintings. And black artists haven't even come close to getting their due. The cover of *American Sublime* is Tanner's *Annunciation,* where the angel Gabriel is not embodied but rather represented as a blazing column of pure light. That use of light I think points to Tanner's interest in the painters of the "American Sublime," but he is also doing something radical by making Gabriel bodiless, therefore raceless (in the late nineteenth century), therefore potentially of any race. Tanner opens up a space of great possibility.

MJ: Your work suggests that our culture needs to have a familiarity with and investment in black visual artists that might come close to how we value our musicians. In African-American poetics a critical turn toward a focus on ekphrasis in poetry and also, more generally, the relationship between visual poetics and visual politics.

EA: Ntozake Shange talked about that when she says in the introduction to *Nappy Edges,* all Chaka would have to do is sing one note and you'd know who it was. She's saying Chaka Khan singing "Empty Bed Blues" is not the same as Bessie Smith singing "Empty Bed Blues," and she goes on like that to say if you are culturally literate about black music, then, it should follow, you should be so literate with the rest of the culture. She's saying, why can't you tell the difference between reading a Nikki Giovanni poem and an Amiri Baraka poem? You don't mix Romare Bearden up with any other artist. You don't. Not if you're paying attention. You don't mix James Brown up with anybody else. How we "sound"—in poems, music, painting—is what we are.

MJ: You mentioned Bearden. There's an illuminating essay by you in the Grant Hill Collection of African American Art catalog, *Something All Our Own,* in which you state, "It's difficult to imagine twentieth-century American art without Romare Bearden" and that his "collage gives us a way to think about the complexities of African American identity." What is Bearden's significance as an individual and an institution? How important is he to *you* in your own writing or might he be for other poets and writers?

EA: Now he's had his big show at the National Gallery and he's on refrigerator magnets and so forth, but it wasn't always so. His career was a career of struggle, of doing different kinds of work, as you know. He was a social worker for a long, long time. He tried to be a songwriter, tried to be a poet. He did a lot of different things. He traveled in the armed services. He was not always that "famous artist." When I wrote about him in my dissertation in the late 1980s there was some scholarship, most notably Mary Schmidt Campbell's dissertation, and there had been some important Bearden shows, but nothing like the kind of availability of and interest in and writing on his work and his images that there is now. As I've written, I think his particular use of the collage as he specifies that technique as African-American—as it engulfs the call and response and jazz improvisation; as it references the Middle Passage and the ripping of something from its original source and reconstituting it in a new space that still has allusions to and memory to that old place—is a brilliant metaphor for talking about black creative production, survival, and living. Also his use of color has always spoken to me very powerfully. That's not just to say that black folk love our bright colors! What I love is that he does not fear the force of color, and he understands the musical power that can be present as it is in the way that he uses color.

There's a lot that is inchoate in how that is part of the poetic process. But nonetheless Bearden's work is deeply part of the bedrock of the process of making poetry for me. He's also personally very important to me because I grew up with his work and with stories about him. Charles "Spinky" Alston, my mother's uncle, was Bearden's cousin. Alston helped Bearden in the New York and Harlem art scene when Bearden came from North Carolina to New York City. One of the Bearden paintings in particular that I grew up with on the wall of my parents' home was a watercolor that he gave to my mother when she was eight years old and he came to Christmas and didn't have any money for store-bought presents, and what I took from that story as a child is something about commitment and the long struggle of an artist.

In college I was writing a paper on his work and I called him up on the phone. I didn't know him, and I asked him to talk about his work and his life. And he said, artists are like mice. They need old houses where no one can bother them and they can just go about their business and do what they have to do. And he said don't do it—that is, become an artist—if you don't have to. I didn't take that as discouragement. Because I guess for me the answer was, well I have to. I try to translate that for my students: be crystal clear about your need to make art. Don't mix it up with trying to get a certain kind of job, or build community, or gain recognition. You can tape up your poems on the wall of a bathroom stall and have more readers than in a literary journal. A carpenter or a ballet dancer understands clearly about perfecting craft, and we who write must also. Why do you do this? Why must you do this? And why must you do this in a way that extends beyond a hobby, something executed with pleasure but not necessarily with devotion. Bearden's "Don't do it if you don't have to" was a very real and necessary statement that I continue to think about and learn from.

I always knew that he was a very well-read and aware person. And that he was an aware black person in the world. And that is to say that being an artist didn't mean, for example, that he didn't have race politics, or that he wouldn't read novels. Perhaps being a great artist is about having many passions and knowledges in excess.

Spinky, who I did know in the family in my childhood before he died, was also a tremendously capacious person. He didn't make it seem like being an artist was about sacrifice, because he was passionate about his work and lucky enough to know what he wanted to devote himself to. As my mother says, well, isn't it good you're not a gymnast because you would have peaked long ago and there'd be nothing you could do about it.

MJ: *(Laughing)* I can imagine Adele Alexander saying that.

EA: Thank goodness I'm doing something I can keep getting better at. I want to connect that back to when we were talking about my work in the college classroom. I want to emphasize that even as we talked about my coming out of that academic world, what I really wanted for *The Black Interior* was for intelligent interested people to be able to pick it up and feel like they had come to be challenged but not shut out by a certain kind of specialized discourse.

MJ: You dedicated *The Black Interior* to Barbara Christian, June Jordan, Toni Cade Bambara, Claudia Tate, Audre Lorde, Sherley Anne Williams—the list continues. You spoke of Elizabeth Catlett before, about her art being on the cover of the book. Why is this lineage of black—diasporically speaking—women artists, critics, writers, and scholars essential to you and your creative work?

EA: What is the institution-building work? And the mentoring work and the breaking-down-the-door work? And the first-black-woman this, that, and the other thing work, that Barbara

Christian did? That means that we don't have fifteen books by her. And she's left this earth. That needs to be spoken and acknowledged. Or the name and example of someone like June Jordan, who was a poet but also who was an institutional and political person. That work is profoundly taxing. It fills you up with other people's words and vibes and energies and struggles. And what do you have to show for it sometimes except that you're tired at the end of the day? Thank God they did the work that they did. But the cautionary lesson is for us to take advantage of the fact that they made it possible for us to make more life-affirming choices. Sometimes *no* is more life-affirming than *yes*. Because for black women in institutions, all that *yes* can eat you up and break you down. Many of these institutions are calcified and wedded to their status quo, and being an empowered and intelligent black person and even more so being an empowered and intelligent and self-respecting black woman is profoundly destabilizing to most status quo. You've got to remember that in a way that's not disabling.

MJ: Think about the debilitating diseases and premature demise of some of the black women writers and artists you list in your dedication for *The Black Interior.* You cannot explicitly say the institution per se caused their untimely deaths. Yet considering cancer, for example, on a metaphysical level, one can sense the limitations of the body's psychic, spiritual, and physical ability to withstand the kind of pressures they had to confront continually. The daily micro-aggressions posed by the sometimes subtle and not so subtle intricacies of racism, sexism, heterosexism, and classism, on an institutional and individual level, undoubtedly affected them, which their writing reflects.

EA: Audre Lorde and June Jordan have given us an important written legacy about cancer and what *that* has to tell us about living in predominantly white institutions—institutions that have not historically welcomed us. Both of those women lived with cancer years longer than anybody expected them to. Even in their writings at least they say that the way they were able to keep fighting and living with it is that they learned to listen to their selves and their bodies, in the face of extreme institutional pressure, of doctors saying, you know, we have to cut it out. I can't even imagine being Audre Lorde and the doctors saying you will die if we don't cut your liver out, and her having the fortitude and self-knowledge and vision to say, I need to approach this another way, there are other ways in the world of thinking about the disease and I'm going to go around the world and learn how other people have dealt with this. That's a metaphor, too. That's a metaphor. What would it mean—what would it mean if all of the black women throughout history and to this day had swallowed and acted upon that which was said about us? We wouldn't have survived. We wouldn't be here.

MJ: Right. In *The Cancer Journals,* Lorde describes her struggle with cancer as "only another face of that continuing battle for self-determination and survival that Black women fight daily, often in triumph." Quite literally, it's what Toni Morrison said in an interview over a decade ago; the marvel is that we're still living. That we *live.* That is the miracle.

EA: I love the late Melvin Dixon's poem "Fingering the Jagged Grain." His work was really important to me and he's talking actually about Bearden in the poem. It concludes: "What did you do? You lived, you lived. With open wings so black and blue, open like mouths about to sing."

MJ: What vibrant lines.

EA: He lived. He lived. Those examples of fierce brilliant, courageous, beautiful, engaged lives full of rampant loving, loving of the word. Loving of the work. Loving of each other. Moving toward what we love and not just toward the destruction of enemies. Now that's what all those women represent to me as well. And that that driving force—that love act—is a force of nature that they believed in. And it empowered them. And that's what I feel like it's important to do upon rising each day.

MJ: And it touches on the power of your essay on *Jet* magazine, this expansive notion of black pride and black loving. In that essay you delineate things concerning *Jet* that you *love*—you use that word—while also articulating other problematic elements in *Jet*. The current institutional moment for black literary and cultural work is different than earlier periods, most prevalently in terms of a queering of black studies that is taking place that is absolutely essential. And this notion of the love act that is not limited to a traditional heterosexual matrix—which isn't saying *that* love act is corrupt and untenable—but instead insisting that there should be a notion of black love and black community that includes men loving men and women loving women, and some loving both, and then all loving in between. So on the one hand, your essay demonstrates the value in black cultural products such as *Jet*, saying, in essence, that what is valuable about *Jet* is that in it black life, even the minutiae of it, *matters* in ways you don't necessarily see manifest in *People* or *Time* magazine. Yet on the other hand you remain ardent in your critique of *Jet*'s limitations. You criticize the narrow vision of black life and black love that has appeared in its pages.

EA: Right. You said it really beautifully. That's what I was trying to get at in that essay. When I was younger I used to think that love as an ethic was—I mean, obviously a good thing, but a little corny. I am certainly an optimist but not a fool. In academic environments, we are taught a skepticism that can lead us to discount the power and force of love. But the older I get, the more I think of all the possible permutations and possibilities of a love ethic. To love someone or something is not just to agree with them or affirm them. To bother to engage with problematic culture, and problematic people within that culture, is an act of love. So what does it mean in a complex and dead-serious way to come from that place of love? If I say, I *love* black people, I love my people, that is not uncritical space, not sentimental. How can that love be useful, echoing Marge Piercy's wonderful poem, "To be of Use"?

MJ: Thinking about that "uncritical space" as a way to talk about black people and black culture, too often we focus on just one individual locale—Harlem, for example, to symbolize the multiplicity of black experience. You were born in New York; yet you grew up in Washington, D.C. Your poetry and prose reflect these richly diverse populations. How does geographical, social, and cultural location influence your work?

EA: As I recently said in a Studio Museum of Harlem publication, "Harlem is my Valhalla." So, yes, I was born there. Yes, that's where my parents come from. And that is an identity as powerful as if they were from, oh, Yugoslavia! They are both from that place, so that necessarily affects who I am and is part of my mythos, an imaginary/real space that I've always been trying to get back to. I think all artists have those spaces or places, those lost childhoods and roads not taken, where versions of ourselves exist. For me, Harlem is an utterly diverse place with everything in it and a rich artistic and political legacy. I think I'm always trying to get back to a party I remember as a child, at my Uncle Spinky's and Aunt Myra's house, where there was jazz, and there was great food, and interesting black people sitting around pontificating and thinking and laughing and I thought this is what I want in my life, period.

With all that said, of course, as you know, being a D.C. sister yourself, Washington is an incredibly diverse and rich and global black place. And it was a wonderful place to grow up. I miss it right at this moment in New England when it's supposed to be springtime and it's not. That D.C. weather put you out on the street for more of the year. You were in contact with other people, and their talk and their walk and their ways. That I really loved growing up. My grandmother was born in Alabama but spent much of her girlhood in Washington. And she—I've written about this in a poem—would go sit on steps of the embassies and just imagine the world. There was the world, the beyond. When she left Washington to go to school, she always said that all her girlfriends came to the train station and just wept. Nobody else was leaving Washington. So she was the adventurer. She became a world traveler. The presence of the embassies and the people from all over the world who worked there was always something that I felt was quite wonderful. I was also intrigued by black Washington's proximity to its southernness. But I didn't realize that until I left how very southern it is. It's all about being interested in how people do things. The *ars poetica* of life. How people talk. And I got to see all of these different ways of being. Also, Washington is a city of free museums. I had to cross town to go to school and I would pass by the museums on the way, get off the bus early, and just go visit "my" paintings.

My father, as you know, ran for mayor of the city, in the first mayoral election held in D.C.—that was '74, so I was twelve. During the campaign just being out in the street with Dad, to the extent that my brother and I were, gave us a political awareness of the city and its issues. We Washingtonians were—and still are—taxed without representation. Home rule is still a struggle not at all unrelated to its being a predominantly black city. It was very inspiring to join hands with people in that political realm as my dad was part of what was also a highly symbolic race for mayor. That is a rare pleasure now in electoral politics.

It was a wonderful place to grow up. I always am very, very happy when I go back there. I think I was probably eighteen or nineteen when I met Ethelbert Miller for the first time and went to his reading room at Howard, and heard stories and saw papers from the many writers he'd known. That is still a rite of passage for young writers in D.C. Sterling Brown, Lois Mailou Jones, Elizabeth Catlett, Alma Thomas, and the color field painters—D.C. has a wonderful cultural history. And for better or worse, D.C. is a black city, and an international black city. We do everything in the city, sometimes beautifully and sometimes not. And I have to say for better or worse *(laughing)*.

MJ: Do you have writing rites? Where and when do you engage the process of composition? Is custom an essential element of the writing life, of your livelihood as a poet?

EA: I try to grab things when I can, to keep notes of things as I internally hear them so that when I do have writing time I have something to begin with.

MJ: Why do you write? What motivates your continual return to your writing desk, your computer? What makes you turn your face toward the blank screen, or ink your ideas onto paper?

EA: Paper first, then the screen, for I feel bollixed up if I don't attend to my internal soundtrack, so there is a personal satisfaction that comes from attending to it in writing. Also, at this point, twenty years into my life as a poet, I feel clearer about having something to say and people who benefit from hearing it.

MJ: Your verse employs a vibrant spectrum of forms and styles: sonnets, sestinas, villanelles, syllabics, accentual-syllabics, free verse, narrative, blues, jazz, ekphrasis, and beyond. Do poems and poetic forms "happen" to you? Which comes first, the subject or the form for a poem? Or, if that's a false dichotomy, what encourages your use of particular forms or styles?

EA: I always tell student poets to read and listen as much and as variously as they can to build up a rolodex of possibilities in their minds when they sit down to write a poem. You always need to have many more possibilities of approaching a poem than you end up using. Walcott would say, "the form will suggest itself to you as you begin the poem," and though I found that mystifying when I first heard it, after many years of practice I now find it is true for me. It's about tuning your internal ear and listening to what the poem at hand is trying to do and be.

MJ: You have published four volumes of poetry, a collection of essays, and a play. Does *American Sublime* signal you are you more at home in the world and rooms and multiple possibilities of form that poetry offers? Or do you have plans to write in other genres, prose fiction, for example in the future? Have you written any verse or stories for children?

EA: I began my life as a creative writer with short fiction, many moons ago. I was lucky enough to study with John Hersey my senior year in college, who helped me find a fictive voice that I now see as compatible with my voice in poetry. I imagine one day I will return to short fiction—many of my poems are "short stories." I have been carrying around an idea for another verse play for a few years now but life with small children is not really compatible with life in the theater. I am in the midst of several more scholarly prose and editorial projects. I have written a book of poems for young adults with Marilyn Nelson, on Prudence Crandall, the nineteenth-century Connecticut teacher who went to extreme lengths to educate young black women. I make up poems and stories for my own children all the time, so I suppose I should put them down on paper. But at the end of the day, the bottom line is that I live centrally in poetry.

MJ: What advice might you give to newer poets and writers concerning the creative process?

EA: Submit to it, tend it, nurture it, honor it. Too may young writers get distracted by thinking about career before process; without process, there is no real work and thus, no career. Every day is another blank page to be filled from your own particular landscape. Process is all.

(2006)

Black Graduates' Celebration

This is a joyous time for you. Your families are proud of you, happy for you, and excited to see what you will do with the time that spills ahead of you like a bolt of gorgeous and variegated cloth. And this is a community's joyous moment as well, the community made up not only of your parents, siblings, grandparents, aunties and uncles and friends, but also all who have encouraged and supported your growth here at Yale. Speaking as one of your teachers, I say that teaching is a devotional act in which we have loved you and learned from you in return and are proud and eager to see what you will do next. As you enter this stage of your lives, you are becoming citizens in a new way, with new responsibilities and possibilities in the communities you come from, choose, and create. And because you are children of the African Diaspora, you have the advantage of a truly great and rich history to teach you as you imagine the future.

I want us to think what it means to be young Americans, young African-Americans, in a time when this country is engaged in an immoral and bankrupt war of aggression wherein young people—some younger than you graduates—are witnessing and participating in the often-unimaginable to serve the will of a short-sighted, megalomaniacal, greed-driven few. People younger than some of you have participated in the humiliation and torture of other human beings in the very name of this country that is ours, no doubt at the behest or with the assent of elders in their chain of command who were entrusted with guiding and setting an example for these very young people in the terrible circumstance of war. It isn't a pleasant topic to bring up at the beginning of a joyous celebration, but it is more than just one topic among many to bring up or sweep under the rug. This war and the American government's lying and dangerous colonial arrogance is ambient and alas not without historical roots and precedents. It is what we are in, it is of the moment of these times that are now yours as you leave the relative security of school and go forth as adult members of society, and alas it reflects on all of us. Whether or not you are originally from the United States and whether or not you plan to live here, you have been educated at one of the country's finest institutions, which as you know produces disproportionate numbers of powerful intellectual and political leaders, so you are all in some key way Americans, black Americans, and you will go forth from Yale University in the world under that sign. What will it mean? What does it mean to you to be African-Americans today?

As black Americans we are lucky that what has been forged from the unique position of our historical relationship to this country is a counter-knowledge, another perspective on Americanness, based on knowing that America has not always been fair, nor made nor kept the same promises to all of her children. Perhaps you were taught to trust the police when Officer Friendly came to your classroom, and no doubt you were taught to respect the law, but you also knew, or you know now, that the police arrested and jailed the likes of Martin Luther King, and abused young children marching for equal civil rights—that good people doing good things have sometimes made the just choice to break the law we are nonetheless taught to respect, and that people in positions of authority are fallible. African-Americans would not have survived without possessing and developing these multiple strands of knowledge that form the critical consciousness we all need to move through the complicated world. More than one kind of knowledge, even when difficult to process, is wealth.

How are you going to define your Americanness? I hope it will be guided by this critical consciousness, by also understanding yourselves as part of the world, as part of an intricate human family, and that when you think of the part that is African-American you will know from whence you sprang—both your crucial individual family history as well as a larger history of African-American people—and strive to think about how that does and does not relate to people of the African Diaspora all over the world. African-Americans are the financially wealthiest black people on the planet, and yet what is it that we need to know and learn about other ways of measuring wealth and value? "Black love is black wealth," wrote Nikki Giovanni in the late 1960s, and love is not sentimental and sweet but tough, knowing, wise, questioning, and ultimately sustaining.

What do you ask of each other? What do I wish for from and for you? I wish for the highest standards of excellence that your families, living and passed on, laid down for you, that got you here, and that you strive to live up to and refashion in the terms of your new now. Some folks lament that black people in predominately white contexts and institutions are expected to work twice as hard, but why not see that as a blessing, as the opportunity to embrace the vitality, commitment, and joy of hard work, and the boon of bountiful knowledge?

Thank the ancestors, for African-Americans are the offspring of people who survived when they were not meant to. And we bloomed. Each of us is a benefactor of that grit, tenacity, and genius of body and spirit, with more than a little good fortune thrown in. Our amazing history and culture are yours to explore, learn, tend, and pass on. Thank your parents: here you are; thank them and everyone who ever loved you and minded you, at home and at school. Thank the people who cleaned up after you and cooked for you to whatever extent, at home and at school. Thank anyone who taught you to do anything for yourself. Thank the people who surprised you with their attention. Thank the teachers who made learning a challenge and encouraged you to do what you were not naturally good at. Thank those who underestimated or mistreated you, for by graduating and coming this far you have decisively proven them wrong, case closed. Racism will not define you nor will it take you down, though you have no doubt experienced it already. In the face of racist words and deeds, my grandmother—reared in the segregated South in the early part of the twentieth century—would say, "Isn't it a pity they are so very limited?" And when I as a young woman told her of racist affronts, she would rhetorically ask, "What does his or her ignorance have to do with you?" Move quickly past these inevitable slights, and do not let the toxins take residence in your psyche. As we began this evening, the world's future is imper-

iled and deeds have been done in the name of our c
will have reverberations for the rest of your lives. H
going to be great Americans, wise and knowing ar
compassionate and humble?

Keep a sound mind in a sound body; always honor
of your bodies by resting to rejuvenate, eating healthfully with
food you have actually prepared, moving your bodies to keep
them maximally strong and enduring and flexible, and by taking
in fresh air and respecting the planet. These ablutions should
be part of your everyday routine. You will be better able to do
what you need to do. You will be stronger and more lucid for the
very real challenges ahead. How can children who begin their
days with the packaged, colored sugar water that is de rigeur in
so many of our schools be expected to be sharp and brilliant and
transcendent if their bodies are hopped up on sucrose at seven-
thirty in the morning? If you respect and honor your own
temple, it only follows that you will extend those actions to those
around you, in your habits of social interaction and sexual union
and in your thinking about those who seem to be far from your
experience.

Speak up and be courageous. Gloria Steinem prescribes that
people commit one outrageous act every day, and I would say,
one courageous act a day, be it an extending act of kindness,
speaking up when the butterflies in our stomach say no, giving
half of your metaphorical sandwich to someone who does not
have one, admitting when you have been wrong, pushing past
where your knowledge stops, through the discomfort of un-
knowing, always speaking truth to power. It was hard for me to
bring some of these words to all the beautiful families gathered
here, because it would have been easier to read celebratory
poems at this time of great celebration. But strong communities
know the most potent and useful challenges come from within.
Only interrogation and challenge from within will make us
stronger and wiser.

Like the old folks say, take someone with you. Now that you
have finished college you have stepped up a level in the age hi-
erarchy in your family and community. There are teenagers and
children who are watching you carefully. Take a younger per-
son—a sibling, a cousin, a neighbor, a friend's child—the next

ume you go to a concert, or to a lecture on a matter of importance. Pass along a book when you have finished with it. Think about the ecosystem of your actions: what you take in, send out, so you have room for more and someone else is filled anew. And take a younger person along when you are doing something mundane so they can see what being a responsible grown-up is all about, when you are doing your errands, paying your bills, gassing the car, shopping for groceries, weeding in the yard, recycling, folding the laundry. These regular acts are as much of what adult life is as the big and shiny moments of career choices and adventure, and when younger people tag along they learn what they need to know to take the next step themselves.

No matter what your discipline or work, support the arts. Listen to what black artists in words, music, dance, or images have to say. The arts may well be the only place where we may envision what we are not meant to envision: "complex black selves, real and enactable black power, rampant and unfetishized black beauty." In a time when the public imagination can be numbing and horrifying in its limitations and constrictions, in art we may find what we need and are hoping for before we have been able to vision, articulate, or enact it. And black artists, who have made the difficult choice of probably limited financial rewards and tough self-investigation, deserve our support and mindfulness. What are we without vision and felicity?

None of us is perfect, nor immune to ignorance and calcified ideology. Learning is a lifetime commitment, and self-knowledge and improvement begins anew each day. Life is full of mighty things but is also hard and humbling. So if we black people have been the conscience of this country, great in so many ways, at times misguided in others, why not continue that? You have seen T-shirts with the slogan "Black to the Future," and you will help define what that future looks like. Let it be better than what speaks the name of this country around the world today. The very critical consciousness of which I have spoken, which DuBois called "double consciousness," which is the mother's milk of Afro-America, is not a burden but a blessing. So engage it. Use it. Meditate from it. Speak on it. Sometimes, preach it. Live fully, and consciously, and, never forget, joyously. There is joy in every day, in simply waking in a body that serves you, to a day full of challenges and possibilities, and people who love you, to hard work and sound rest. Each ion of joy and kindness we put out into the world countermands the extreme violence that rends this planet. So living joyously is a dead-serious choice that I believe is our only choice, and in that choice, joy, is infinite possibility.

Nostalgia is not to be confused with real historical consciousness, but it certainly is pleasurable. So permit me just a brief moment of site-specific nostalgia. Next week, after you are gone, I will attend my twentieth Yale College reunion. I have been in your shoes, your very cap and gown in this very spot. I think every day about the grandmother I quoted earlier, who watched me graduate but has been gone for ten years. Her insights are pithier and more necessary to me as the years go by. Learn from and honor your loved ones. They will always be with you, but treasure them when they are by your side. And as I graduated, I did not know that I had found my life's work, the study of African-American literature and culture, the teaching of it, and my own writing, that I had already found my life's work right here, in this community. Who knew, as I moved from city to city over the years, that this was where I would land? My point is, this place is your place, in ways you might not imagine or know right now. Let that be a resource to you. And may you live up to the privilege of your education with continued and ever-developing knowledge, wisdom, compassion, generosity, justice, and once again, joy.

(2005)

Africa and the World

I've been asked, very loosely, to think about the relationship of African writers and Africa, writ large, to American writing.

Even before 1922, when the African-American poet Countee Cullen wrote his famous poem "Heritage," Africa was a monolith, an idea, for most Americans. We know that through the idea of Africa, white Americans have found their imagined antithesis, their trilled fantasies. Even or perhaps especially in children's literature, one still encounters vulgar stereotypes such as bones through the nose, wild-eyed savages, and darling naifs in contemporary garb. America's beloved monkey Curious George is happy to be captured from Africa and kept in the lovely zoo in America.

But what of the African-American writer's relationship to her African predecessors and peers? That, for me, is a richer question. In "Heritage," Cullen wrote: "What is Africa to me? Copper sun or scarlet sea?" He echoed William Blake's metrical and rhyme patterns in "The Tyger" ("Tyger Tyger, burning bright, / In the forests of the night; / What immortal hand or eye, / Could frame thy fearful symmetry?") in writing the African-American self relative to the imagined African self. For "Africa," as such, was no more real or known to Cullen than to Picasso when he first saw those sculptures in Paris in 1913 and was so radically rocked at the aesthetic and philosophical root that his entire artistic project—and European art history—changed forever. We know from the landmark 1925 anthology *The New Negro,* edited by Alain Locke, that many African-Americans were seeing and imagining Africa for the first time when these art and artifacts made their way to the Western world. So Africa was for them also a fantasy, and their relationship to it, open for exploration and investigation.

And yet, and yet. The African-American has a different history, a different melancholia that comes from the interruption, the violent fissure of the Middle Passage and its subsequent soul-annihilating indignities. That melancholia is about the never-to-be-resolved fissure and the never-to-be-known homeland that coexists with the great possibilities of reinvention that gave the world, for example, jazz, a music that is heavily influenced by African music but utterly, yes, purely, completely, African-American, which is to say American, and the whole idea of double consciousness as it plays out through the century, and the unique aspects of our history and then something, something never reachable. Our death is at the bottom of the ocean and then at the hands of the brutal slave system and then due to the privations of Jim Crow and then at the hands of the police and of each other. That's a lot of unending blues.

I think of Gwendolyn Brooks's wonderful words: "I am a black. I am one of the Blacks. We occur everywhere. Don't call me out of my name," and her wish that to be called black links her to other African people, diasporized and not. Does that linkage hold? Is our wish for it to hold sentimental? What is the motherland that each of us may wish for and what does it mean to try to heal that? Art historian Robert Farris Thompson called these "African retentions," our bottle trees and shell-studded graves. In our poetry, it is the continued effort of black American poets of almost all stripes to keep the ear open, both for the literal sounds of Englishes and an oral tradition, whatever is left of proverbial logic and structure, and also for the mythos, for the African something. Now we send our cheek scrapings and hair strands to Howard University to the genomic projects that we hope will tell us—not so much how much of what we have in us but rather a name: Fulani, Hausa, Ibo, Kissi, Luo—that will tell us something about what we come from, give us something to start with. In that search for roots, do we overlook that which we have, skip right over to the easier work of romance and iconography? Perhaps we overlook what we have and have already made, and the added challenges of being an American in the world, with civic responsibilities to have our say in our country's role at home and in the world. In grappling with the literary possibilities of reality, trying to bring the spoken word into the written form, true African-American genius has bloomed.

I think also about moments of contact and cross-pollination: the mutual admiration society between Toni Morrison and Chinua Achebe; the relationship the late poet and scholar Melvin Dixon had to Senegal and his fine, definitive translation of the complete poems of Senghor; Langston Hughes's anthologies of African short stories and poems that brought African writers to African readers in the 1950s and early 1960s, Robert Hayden's winning the Grand Prix for literature at the world festival of black arts in Darar in 1966. Dizzy Gillespie gives a trumpet to the young Hugh Masakela; Stevie Wonder and Sounds of Distinction cover Masakela's "Grazin' in the Grass"; James Brown and Fela Kuti riff back and forth, endlessly and fiercely.

For many of us of my generation, the anti-apartheid movement was a way to connect with African issues. It was a sometimes violent civil rights struggle, a battle for desegregation and human dignity that resonated with our own history. In a time in the United States when affirmative action battles were in order and the Reagan era was changing the country's winds from the Great Society of the 1960s, the "Free South Africa Movement" kept our eyes on the prize when the struggle was hoped to be over. The rhetoric was at hand and the issues in the anti-apartheid movement were blissfully clear. Clarity about one's issues is a gift to the young and the struggling.

How do we live in fruitful contact with the ancestral aspects of our cultures while living in and up to the demands of globalization and its cultural analogue of a multiculturalism that aspires to cuteness rather than depth and challenge? This of course takes us to today, to the population of young black people like the ones I teach, who are as likely to have been born in Lagos or Port of Spain as in Los Angeles. The diaspora is alive and well and has a new face. The black kids are now—as my own children, whose father is from Eritrea, describe themselves, "Mommy, you're African-American but we're Aaaafrican-American." So the Eritrean student who was born and raised in Addis Ababa until the latest round of the Ethio-Eritrean war and is now a student at a Midwestern college finds herself in conversation with the black kids who don't know a thing about her background. We have contemporary writers who are both African and American such as Meri Nana-Amah Danquah and Uzodinma Iweala, a whole generation of twenty-somethings who I know we are going to hear from in large numbers. It is the literature I'm looking for.

Being a race warrior, worker, or even just a scholar in the American context is exhausting work. Sometimes the mind's portals fill up and may seem unresponsive to the necessary knowledges that await under African skies. I say without hesitation that from African people and African literature we have learned certain essential aspects of these large categories: beauty, grace, patience, woe, and joy. There is more for us to find, for the width of the African sky to expand within us here in the United States of America.

(2005)

Notes

THE GENIUS OF ROMARE BEARDEN

1. *Romare Bearden, 1911–1988: A Memorial Exhibition* (New York: ACA Galleries, 1989), 3.

2. W. E. B. DuBois, *The Souls of Black Folk*, in *W. E. B. DuBois*, ed. Nathan Huggins (New York: Library of America, 1986), 364–65.

3. Ralph Ellison, "The Art of Romare Bearden," in *Going to the Territory* (New York: Random House, 1986), 234.

4. Pablo Picasso in conversation with Francoise Gilot, quoted in Marjorie Perloff, "The Invention of Collage," in *Collage* (New York: New York Literary Forum, 1983), 5–47.

5. *Romare Bearden: Origins and Progressions* (Detroit: Detroit Institute of Arts, 1986), 41.

6. John Michael Vlach, *The Afro-American Tradition in Decorative Arts* (Athens: University of Georgia Press, 1990), 45–48. See also Gladys-Marie Fry, *Stitched from the Soul: Slave Quilts in the Ante-Bellum South* (New York: Dutton Studio Books, 1990); Robert Farris Thompson, "Round Houses and Rhythmic Textiles: Mande-Related Art and Architecture in the Americas," in *His Flash of the Spirit: African and Afro-American Art and Philosophy* (New York: Random House, 1983), 193–224; Maude Southwell Wahlman and John Scully, "Aesthetic Principles in Afro-American Quilts," in *Afro-American Folk Arts and Crafts*, ed. William Ferris (Jackson: University Press of Mississippi, 1983), 79–97; and Alvia Wardlaw's introduction to John Beardsley et al., *The Quilts of Gee's Bend* (Atlanta: Tinwood, 2002).

7. Herta Wescher, *Collage* (New York: Harry N. Abrams, 1972), 8.

8. Eddie Wolfram, *History of Collage: An Anthology of Collage, Assemblage and Event Structure* (New York: Macmillan, 1975), 7.

9. Gregory Ulmer, "The Object of Post-Criticism," in *The Anti-Aesthetic: Essays on Post-Modern Culture*, ed. Hal Foster (Seattle: Bay Press, 1983), 84.

10. Claude Lévi-Strauss, *The Savage Mind* (Chicago: University of Chicago Press, 1966), 17.

11. Bearden, *A Memorial Exhibition*, 21. This is the earliest published Bearden collage that I have found, though it is possible that others exist in private collections or family papers.

12. *Ten Hierographic Paintings by Sgt. Romare Bearden* (Washington, D.C.: G Place Gallery, 1944).

13. Mary Schmidt Campbell writes: "In 1964, [Bearden] abruptly abandoned his nonobjective oil paintings . . . when he began making his collages. . . . Having lived with a number of different ideas of art, he had come back to the subject matter he started out with—Black American life as he remembered it in the South of his childhood in North Carolina, and in the North of his coming of age in Pittsburgh and Harlem, and, later in life, the Caribbean island of St. Martin." *Memory and Metaphor: The Art of Romare Bearden, 1940–1987* (New York: Studio Museum in Harlem, 1991), 8.

THE YELLOW HOUSE ON THE CORNER AND BEYOND

1. Helen Vendler, "An Interview with Rita Dove," in *Reading Black, Reading Feminist: A Critical Anthology,* ed. Henry Louis Gates, Jr. (New York: Meridian, 1990), 485.

2. This paper quotes from the following of Rita Dove's collections of poetry: *The Yellow House on the Corner* (Pittsburgh: Carnegie-Mellon University Press, 1980); *Museum* (Pittsburgh: Carnegie-Mellon University Press, 1983); *Thomas and Beulah* (Pittsburgh: Carnegie-Mellon University Press, 1986), and *Grace Notes* (New York: W. W. Norton, 1989). Further citations will be made parenthetically.

3. Stan Sanvel Rubin and Earl G. Ingersoll, "A Conversation with Rita Dove," in *Black American Literature Forum* 20, no. 3 (1986): 53–60.

4. In *The Writer on Her Work.*

5. Steven Schneider, "Coming Home: An Interview with Rita Dove," *Iowa Review* 19, no. 3 (1989): 118.

MY GRANDMOTHER'S HAIR

1. See Marita Bonner's 1925 essay "To Be Young, a Woman, and Colored," for one meditation on these questions. Bonner entered Radcliffe College in 1918 and no doubt knew Caroline Bond Day. Her essay is reprinted in *Marita Bonner, Frye Street and Environs: The Collected Works of Marita Bonner,* ed. Joyce Flynn (Boston: Beacon Press, 1989), 3–8.

2. See Lee D. Baker, *From Savage to Negro: Anthropology and the Construction of Race, 1896–1954* (Berkeley and Los Angeles: University of California Press, 1998), for a discussion of how anthropologists have contributed to the formation of racial categories; and Ira E. Harrison and Faye V. Harrison, eds., *African-American Pioneers in Anthropology* (Urbana: University of Illinois Press, 1999), for essays about important African-American figures in the field and a genealogy of their participation in and exclusion from the discipline.

3. As quoted in Adele Logan Alexander, *Homelands and Waterways. The American Journey of the Bond Family, 1846–1926* (New York: Pantheon, 1999), 377.

"IMITATIONS OF LIFE"?

1. Patricia Hill Collins, *Black Feminist Thought: Knowledge, Consciousness, and the Politics of Empowerment* (London: Routledge, 1990), 71.

2. Chester W. Pierce et al., "An Experiment in Racism: TV Commercials," *Education and Urban Society* 10, no. 1 (1977): 61–88.

"COMING OUT BLACKENED AND WHOLE"

1. "An Interview with Audre Lorde," interview by Karla Hammond, *American Poetry Review,* March–April 1980, 8.

2. "Audre Lorde: An Interview," interview by Karla Hammond, *Denver Quarterly* 16 (1981): 15.

3. Audre Lorde, *Zami: A New Spelling of My Name* (Freedom: Crossing Press, 1984), 25. Subsequent citations are given in the text.

4. Interview by Claudia Tate, in *Black Women Writers at Work,* ed. Claudia Tate (New York: Continuum, 1983), 104.

5. Interview by Tate, 102.

6. Audre Lorde, "A Burst of Light: Living with Cancer," in *A Burst of Light: Essays* (Ithaca, N.Y.: Firebrand, 1988), 76–77. Subsequent citations are given in the text.

7. Audre Lorde, *The Cancer Journals* (San Francisco: Spinsters, 1980), 14–15. Subsequent citations are given in the text.

8. For example, Bearden cuts paper in identifiable iconographic shapes such as the arc of a watermelon slice, the ruffle of a rooster comb, curls of steam engine smoke, or the shape of a guitar. Each of these has specific meaning in Bearden's African-American cosmology.

9. Gerda Lerner, ed., *Black Women in White America: A Documentary History* (New York: Vintage-Random, 1973), 163–64.

10. Audre Lorde, "Uses of the Erotic: The Erotic as Power," in *Sister Outsider: Essay and Speeches* (Freedom: Crossing Press, 1984), 54.

11. See Sander L. Gilman, "Black Bodies, White Bodies: Toward an Iconography of Female Sexuality in Late Nineteenth-Century Art, Medicine, and Literature," in *"Race," Writing, and Difference,* ed. Henry Louis Gates, Jr. (Chicago: University of Chicago Press, 1986), 232–35.

12. "An Interview with Audre Lorde," interview by Adrienne Rich, *Signs* 6 (1981): 715.

13. James Alan McPherson, "The Story of a Scar," in *Elbow Room: Stories* (Boston: Little, Brown, 1972), 97. Subsequent citations are given in the text.

14. Terrie S. Rouse, "Howardena Pindell: Odyssey," in *Howardena Pindell: Odyssey* (New York: Studio Museum in Harlem, 1986), 8.

15. Howardena Pindell, lecture, Philadelphia Museum of Art, April 15, 1991.

MEMORY, COMMUNITY, VOICE

1. Robert Vasquez-Pacheco, in *Sojourner: Black Gay Voices in the Age of AIDS,* ed. B. Michael Hunter (New York: Other Countries, 1993), 81.

2. Marlon Riggs, in Hunter, *Sojourner,* 20.

Acknowledgments

"Dunbar Lives!"
From a paper given at the Paul Laurence Dunbar Conference, Stanford University, March 12, 2006.

"Sterling Brown: Where Academic Meets Vernacular"
From the *Village Voice Literary Supplement* (May 1990).

"Nerudiana"
From a lecture given at the Pablo Neruda Centennial Celebration, Santiago, Chile, January 2004.

"Ode to Miss Gwendolyn Brooks: (Ten Small Serenades)"
From *Black Issues Book Review* (November–December 2000).

"The Genius of Romare Bearden"
From *Something All Our Own: The Grant Hill Collection of African-American Art,* ed. Alvia Wardlaw (Duke University Press 2003).

"Lucille"
From a lecture given at the Poetry Society of America tribute to Lucille Clifton, November 2004.

"Living in Americas: Poems by Victor Hernández Cruz"
From the *Village Voice Literary Supplement,* November 1991.

"The One Who Went Before and Showed the Way: Remembering August Wilson"
From *American Scholar,* Winter 2006.

"Bill T. Jones *Still/Here*"
From the *Walker Art Center Catalogue,* in connection with the Bill T. Jones performance *As I was saying . . .* (2005).

"My Grandmother's Hair"
The Black Body, ed. Meri Nana-Amah Danquah (Norton, 2007).

"'Imitations of Life'? A Very Short History of Black Women and Food in Popular Iconography from Jemima to Oprah, or, When Is a Pancake Not Just a Pancake?"
From a paper given at the Modern Language Association convention, 1992.

"'Coming Out Blackened and Whole': Fragmentation and Reintegration in Audre Lorde's *Zami* and *The Cancer Journals*"
From *American Literary History,* Winter 1994.

"Black Alive and Looking Straight at You: The Legacy of June Jordan"
From the Poetry Foundation website, Fall 2006.

"Memory, Community, Voice"
From a paper given at the Black Women in the Academy conference (1992). Versions of the essay were later published in the *Women's Review of Books,* February 1994, and in *Callaloo,* Spring 1996.

"Kitchen Table Blues"
From the *Village Voice Literary Supplement,* October 1995.

"A Conversation with Deborah Keenan and Diane LeBlanc"
From *Water-Stone Review,* Fall 2003.

"Who Is the Self in Language? / Rooted in Language: An Interview with Meta DuEwa Jones"
From the *AWP Chronicle,* Fall 2006.

"Black Graduates' Celebration"
From the commencement speech given at Yale University, Battell Chapel, June 1995.

"Africa and the World"
From a paper given at the PEN International Writer's Conference, April 2005.

UNDER DISCUSSION
David Lehman, General Editor
Donald Hall, Founding Editor

Volumes in the Under Discussion series collect reviews and essays about individual poets. The series is concerned with contemporary American and English poets about whom the consensus has not yet been formed and the final vote has not been taken. Titles in the series include: